CHAIRMEN OF THE BOARDS

BILL GUTMAN

tempo
books
GROSSET & DUNLAP
A Filmways Company
Publishers • New York

ACKNOWLEDGMENTS

The author would like to thank the following people for their help in providing background material and information useful in the preparation of this book:

Matt Winick and his staff at National Basketball Association headquarters, the public relations departments of the Houston Rockets and Boston Celtics; Greg Jennings at Indiana State University, and the sports information department at Michigan State University.

CHAIRMEN OF THE BOARDS:
ERVING, BIRD, MALONE, JOHNSON

Photos of Larry Bird and Julius Erving by
  Mitchell B. Reibel/FOCUS ON SPORTS

Photos of Moses Malone and Magic Johnson by
  FOCUS ON SPORTS

Copyright © 1980 by Bill Gutman
All Rights Reserved
ISBN: 0-448-17201-1
A Tempo Books Original
Tempo Books is registered in the U.S. Patent Office
Printed in the United States of America
Published simultaneously in Canada

JULIUS ERVING

JUST DROP THE NAME of "the Doctor" to any basketball fan and you'll get instant recognition. No one is about to ask, "Doctor Who?" or question you with a "Who's that?" It isn't necessary. Though some still refer to him as Doctor J or just plain Doc, the Doctor is only one man—Julius Erving. Erving is the all-star forward for the Philadelphia 76ers, and in the minds of many, he's the most electrifying front courtman ever to play professional basketball.

Sports' insiders have known about the Doctor ever since he hit the American Basketball Association in 1971. That year he averaged 27 points a game as a rookie for a team called the Virginia Squires.

To many basketball purists, the ABA wasn't really a pro league, just a four-year-old pretender that could never be on a par with the older, established National Basketball Association. So, even when Julius was traded to the ABA New York Nets, he still wasn't considered big time. In 1974 and 1976, his magic enabled the Nets to win a pair of ABA titles. By then the league was ready to fold and already off national television, which led one writer to say, "For years, he [Julius] was the least known, or least seen, great athlete performing in America."

There was a great deal of truth to that although the Doctor didn't get any national headlines as a collegian. It wasn't that he lacked talent, that was always there in abundance. He didn't seek collegiate court glory and the assurance of a big start to his pro career. Instead, the Doctor, attended the University of Massachusetts, which didn't play a major college hoop schedule, but offered him the kind of atmosphere and environment he felt was best for his all-around growth and enjoyment.

Julius Erving was a self-assured, controlled young man, and it didn't really bother him when he wasn't touted as an all-American, the greatest this or the greatest that. He knew he was as good as the others, and later he even made a joke out of it.

"I caught everybody by surprise," he said, "and that helped. No one was sick of reading about how great I was in college and, more importantly, no one knew my moves."

Knowing the Doctor's moves wouldn't have helped anyway. At 6 ft. 7 in. tall and 215 pounds, Julius is blessed with great leaping ability, huge hands, and an uncanny instinct for the game. His inside game was always incredible. When the Doctor operated near the hoop, he was almost impossible to stop. Using his leaping ability and amazing body control, he would often hang in the air longer than defenders, twisting, turning, pumping, faking, then hitting miraculous shots from all angles. When given an inch of daylight, the Doctor can slam-dunk like no one else in the game.

But despite his enormous natural skills, the Doctor hasn't always experienced smooth sailing as a pro. While leading the Nets to the top of the ABA, Julius put on a dazzling show almost every night, and was especially devastating in the playoffs. But that was the ABA and all the aforementioned criticisms applied.

Prior to the 1976-77 season, the ABA folded, and four of its teams, including the Nets, were taken into the NBA. At last, the Doctor would be able to show his stuff to the entire basketball world and on national television at that. Unfortunately, it didn't work out that way. Julius ran into contract problems with the club and before the season started, he was sold to the Philadelphia 76ers.

The Sixers felt they were building a title team. They had a number of talented players plus one of the best forwards in the game—George McGinnis. Suddenly, Julius wasn't the main man anymore. But that was fine with him since being part of a winning team was always more important to him. The problem was that more often than not, the Sixers didn't play like a team, but like a bunch of individuals looking for their own shots and stats. There just weren't enough basketballs to go around, and not much of a chance for the Doctor to show the kind of basketball that made him an ABA legend.

"For me to sit in the stands and watch his game go down the way it did hurt me more than I've ever been hurt," said Julius' wife, Turquoise. "It was like being married to an executive who had been demoted."

There were flashes now and then, enough to

make fans hungry for more, but it wasn't until the 1978-79 season, when the Sixers began changing the face of the team, that the *old* Doctor began to emerge. The Sixers became Julius' team in 1979-80. Then he was the leader and the team finally played together, both offensively and defensively. And when the club needed a hoop in a pinch, it was the Doctor who got the ball.

So, in a sense, it took nearly eight years for Julius Erving to get complete recognition as a great pro. But during all that time, the Doctor never complained, never sulked, never promoted himself the way many of today's athletes often do. He was always a consummate professional, friendly, frank, candid, and cooperative with fans and the media, all this serving to make him not only one of the finest athletes in the sport, but one of the most popular as well.

Julius Winfred Erving was born on February 22, 1950, in East Meadow, New York, and spent most of his early years in nearby Hempstead. Both towns are located on Long Island, which is very near New York City. He had a sister and brother, and the three children were raised primarily by Mrs. Erving since Julius' parents separated when he was just three years old.

The family lived in a four-story housing project in Hempstead and Mrs. Erving provided for her children by working hard as a domestic. She also tried to give her children the right values and succeeded in keeping them out of trouble, something that was no easy task in the poor neighborhood.

"Julius' mother was the prime reason he turned out to be such a good kid," recalls Don Ryan, a high school teacher who ran a basketball program at the Salvation Army Youth Center in Hempstead. "She worked very hard and Julius copied her. When he was old enough, he was out delivering morning newspapers from 4 to 8 a.m. every day. He got it all from her."

Don Ryan met the young Doctor when Julius was ten. Until then, Julius had played most of his basketball at Campbell Park, which was right next to his home. He didn't take the game too seriously then, but showed enough natural talent to be recommended for Don Ryan's Salvation Army team, which was for boys from ten to twelve years old. When he heard it was a real team, complete with uniforms, young Julius jumped at the chance.

He soon found that in Don Ryan he had not only a coach, but a man who would have a profound influence on the rest of his life.

"Don Ryan took a complete interest in us as boys, not only as ballplayers," Julius recalls. "A lot of the guys who played for him came from broken homes and he taught us many of the things we probably would have learned from our fathers.

"He was very helpful, for instance, in giving me a positive view of life. I had grown up never knowing I was from the other side of the tracks, but when I started to look around and see the way other people lived, I asked Don what I had to do so that I would have a choice. He told me flat out that I would have to perform in school the way I did on the basketball court. It was something I never forgot. Unfortunately, many of the other people I played with, excellent ballplayers, just couldn't do that and some of them suffered for it later in their lives."

There was also the continued strength Julius got

from his family, the closeness that had evolved between his mother, brother, and sister.

"We survived as a family because of determination and a very positive outlook," he says. "There were quite a few people who I grew up with that had the same kinds of opportunities, but not the same attitude. They thought they'd just do nothing like everybody else, hang around all the time and that would be it. What they didn't realize was that goals determine what you're going to be."

It didn't take Julius long to figure out that his goals should include basketball. The Salvation Army team traveled all over Long Island, allowing him to see places he had never seen before, and giving him visions of even greater things down the road.

"I slowly began to see that basketball represented an avenue for getting away and seeing things," he said, "and the more I saw the more I wanted to see. In fact, before long I wanted to see it all!"

Julius worked hard for the three years he played for Don Ryan's team. Both his game and his outlook improved. He was a talented and bright youngster, and he worked very hard both at basketball and his schoolwork, as well as working whenever he could to help support the family.

When he was 13, his life changed. His mother remarried and the family moved to Roosevelt, which wasn't far from Hempstead. As soon as he moved, Julius sought the nearest basketball court, which was located at the Roosevelt Park playground. It didn't take long for him to make friends and begin playing there regularly. He quickly showed that he was just about the best player of his age in the area.

When he went to Roosevelt High he became the star of the freshman basketball team, and before the season was over, he was moved up to the Varsity team. He was a starter as a sophomore, a thin 5 ft. 10 in., but he already had very large hands and was beginning to grow quickly. For a time, his coach at Roosevelt, Ray Wilson, wondered just how tall he'd be.

But Julius did begin to grow. As a junior in 1966 –67, he was beginning to creep over 6 ft. and he had a great season, leading the Roosevelt team into the Nassau County playoffs. Though they didn't win, Julius played extremely well under pressure, a trait that would carry with him right into college and then the pros.

It was also about this time that he got the nickname that would also stay with him, though many people think he acquired it much later. It was simply the result of his friends beginning to tag each other with nicknames.

"Some of the guys even named themselves," Julius recalls. "I remember one guy starting to call himself the Professor, and before long I was the Doctor. I guess it stuck. It wasn't until I turned pro with Virginia that they started using Doctor J, but the Doctor goes way back to Roosevelt High."

As the Doctor, Julius already knew that basketball was a good prescription for a number of things. For one, there was the business of his future.

"I knew by then I had talent, that I could play the game," he says, "so I also knew that basketball could help get me somewhere. Yet at that time I didn't think of it in terms of pro ball. It was one step at a time, I guess, and then the biggest thing I felt basketball could do for me was help me get a good education."

That was the long range prescription as the Doctor saw it, and there was also a short-term one, which he used whenever he felt it was necessary.

"If I had a problem at home, or even one in school or on the streets, I didn't let it get the best of me or take it out on someone or something else. I'd simply go over to the playground and look for a game, which always enabled me to work the other things out of my system. It certainly beat yelling and screaming all over the place."

Coach Wilson concurred with this, saying, "Julius took out all his natural aggressions on the basketball court rather than in a less socially acceptable place."

When Julius returned to Roosevelt for his senior year he was nearly 6 ft. 3½ ins. tall, and though he weighed just 165 pounds, he already had great body control and surprising strength. The leaping ability was always there and so was the knowledge. "I knew what the game was about," says the Doctor. He took off from the first game and began putting together a great season, averaging about 25 points a game, and despite going underneath against bigger, bulkier boys, he grabbed some seventeen rebounds a game.

Though Julius didn't garner any national headlines as a high school hotshot, it wasn't long before the college scouts and recruiters discovered his talents. He began getting phone calls and letters, followed by invitations for campus visits and the various promises made in the cutthroat business of college recruiting. As usual, the Doctor stayed cool and level-headed, and didn't get swept away by the adulation that was being heaped upon him.

"When I started getting all those offers," he said, "I decided the best thing for me to do was make a little trip and take a look at some places first hand. So I went out West and visited Iowa State and Ohio State. I didn't really like either place and after giving the whole thing some more thought, I decided to stay in the East."

"There were several good city schools that I might have enjoyed," he said, "but I figured there would be too many distractions in the city. I was very much interested in getting a good education and becoming a better basketball player at the same time. Soon, I began looking to the New England area."

The schools the Doctor began looking at were not known for their basketball programs, in other words, their teams weren't among the major college powers. They were colleges such as Dartmouth, Amherst, Boston University, Rhode Island, Connecticut, and the University of Massachusetts. Pretty soon, he began leaning toward Massachusetts, which was located at Amherst, Massachusetts.

"I visited there several times," he recalls, "and I liked the campus very much. The school had a fine academic reputation and the basketball program seemed to be on the upswing. I felt I'd have a good chance to start as a sophomore, but more importantly, I knew that basketball did not come before academics and at that time I just wanted to play somewhere and enjoy it while I got my education. My philosophy was that if a ballplayer is good enough to make it, he'll make it, and it won't matter if he's at the University of Massachusetts or UCLA."

Perhaps the final straw was the fact that Ray Wilson was a friend of the University of Massachusetts coach, Jack Leaman, and that gave Julius an extra sense of trust in the entire situation. "I knew I wouldn't be used there," was the way Julius put it. "I trusted the people."

So the Doctor had made his decision, and although it surprised many people, he stuck with it. Some of the big time schools thought they could get him to change his mind, but he wouldn't budge. He finished high school on a high note, satisfied and optimistic about the future, but before he left for his freshman year at the University of Massachusetts, tragedy struck.

Julius' younger brother, Marvin, had contracted a rare disease, and within three months of developing it, he died, a huge loss to the close-knit family. It was part of a whole chain of events that occurred in a short period of time which had a profound effect on Julius, but eventually a positive one.

"My brother's death was on my mind a lot, still is," he said, sometime later. "The family was always close and my mother had always worked very hard to make us all comfortable. But during that period everything changed very quickly. Marvin died and my sister got married. Then I went away to college. Suddenly my mother was without kids for the first time. I thought back to that period quite often and I guess I always pushed a little harder because of it."

So Julius didn't enter college in the fall of 1968 on a particularly high note. His brother's death was too recent, but he still knew he had an important opportunity and he was determined to make the most of it. He buckled down to his studies immediately and also played as much ball as he could, getting ready for his first campaign.

So the Doctor was very purposeful and as soon as he began performing with the freshman team, everyone around the campus knew he was something special. The freshman games were played before the Varsity games and usually played to near-empty houses. The fans would begin trickling in during the second half in anticipation of the varsity . . . that is, until Julius arrived. Suddenly, capacity crowds were turning out to see the University of Massachusetts frosh, and some of the people were actually leaving before the Varsity team came on the floor.

The reason was the Doctor. He was giving everybody a treat even before the game began. In the warm-ups, he'd go through a variety of incredible slam-dunk shots that would have the crowd screaming and cheering in disbelief. Once, after he went high over the rim for a two-handed, over-the-head slam, he got a standing ovation, and the game hadn't started yet.

He was just as good when the action began, dazzling opponents with his moves and leaping ability. Led by Julius, the freshman team began ripping through its opponents. Then on February 22, 1969, Julius took to the floor for a game and all the fans suddenly stood and sang Happy Birthday to him. He was 19 years old that night and everyone made it a night he wouldn't forget.

"Nothing like that had ever happened to me before. I got goose bumps all over. It was a tremendously exciting thing."

When the season ended, the freshman team was unbeaten for the first time in its history, and everyone could hardly wait for the next season to begin, for the Doctor would then be operating with the Varsity.

By the time the 1969-70 season was set to begin, Julius was nearly at his full height of 6 ft. 7 ins. tall. He could already do uncanny things around the basket, and although the dunk shot was outlawed in games at that time, he was still the most exciting player in New England. Of course, the rest of the country knew nothing about him then, but that didn't bother the Doctor, and University of Massachusetts fans were thankful that he was their very own.

With the Doctor in the lineup the Minutemen became a winning team, though not a great one. Julius was far and away the top talent on the club and there wasn't a great deal of depth. Not many players of Erving's caliber would opt for a school such as Massachusetts. The call to the big time was just too great. But the Doctor was always different, as his high school coach, Ray Wilson, recalled, as he followed Julius' career at the University of Massachusetts.

"Julius always personified class," Wilson said. "In high school he was one of the boys, but even in their presence he knew how to relate to different age groups. I'm not saying he was an angel, but if my son can make the transition from adolescence to manhood the way Julius did, I'll be the happiest man in the world."

The Minutemen continued to win most of their games, and Julius kept shining, ringing up impressive numbers. Since the slam-dunk was outlawed in college ball, the Doctor had to get that phase of his game out of the way in the warm-ups, putting on a great show for the early fans, and there were plenty of them. Julius had been able to palm a basketball since he was in the seventh grade and began dunking on an eight-foot basket about a year later. So his ability to stuff the ball was already highly refined.

During games, of course, he had to control himself and shoot regulation lay-ups. He also had to restrict his desire to run and fastbreak, the kind of game generally played in the playgrounds and schoolyards of the big cities. There was just not enough top talent in the college team to play that kind of fast-paced game. Instead the club played a deliberate, slow-down game, setting up plays and running them with patience. But Julius never complained. He looked for the positive and later said that his college games gave him additional court discipline and enabled him to learn some additional technical points of the game. Ray Wilson also commented on the way the Doctor adjusted to the play at University of Massachusetts.

"The whole playground thing is a means of expression for black kids," Wilson said. "It's a way of getting their peers' approval, the moment of one-on-one, where a guy takes a challenge and beats his man. With black kids, life is a struggle for pride, so second best is nothing. You've got to establish yourself as number one and the playgrounds are one way of doing it.

"But again, Julius was different. He didn't have those hang-ups. I remember when he was a junior in high school. He didn't start for me right away, even though he had to know he was the best player I had. Most kids in that situation would have quit, because they would have felt their friends thought them fools for doing all that practicing just to play second string.

"Yet Julius was always self-confident. He knew how good he was and didn't have to brag about it or prove it. So to change his game at the University was easy for him."

Julius looked at it in a slightly different light, though he echoed much of what Ray Wilson said about the playground style and psychology.

"I grew rather slowly, but always had big hands and could jump," Julius said, "so I learned early to be trickier than the bigger guys. I always liked to experiment and loved to watch what other guys would do in emergency situations. Doing all that, I slowly learned to use what I had to the greatest advantage. I set no dimensions for my game and decided early not to limit myself, especially when I realized I could do anything I'd ever seen any other guy do.

"You're forced to do some of this when you compete on the playgrounds. There's a whole psychology that makes you want to beat a guy, beat him in a way that makes him pay twice. You want to outscore him and you also want to freak him out with a big move or a big block.

"That's the kind of thinking that used to dominate my mind in informal game situations, but I feel I've never let it become part of my concept of how a formal, five-man game should be played. If a guy can't break the playground mold when he has to, it's going to restrict his usefulness and eventually his game."

So the Doctor did what he had to do to fit in with his teammates, yet help them win at the same time. He played a team game, but when it became necessary for him to go one-on-one, he did it in ways that left everyone gaping in awe. There seemed to be no end to the different kinds of moves he made. When the 1969–70 season ended, the Minutemen had an 18–6 record, best in the school's history, and the Doctor had set a slew of individual school marks.

Playing in 25 games including a post-season contest, he scored 643 points for a 25.7 average, best in the Yankee Conference. He also grabbed 522 rebounds, giving him a remarkable 20.9 rebounding average, which not only led the Yankee Conference, but was the second best mark in the entire nation. The only player to top the Doctor in rebounds was a 7 ft. 2 in. giant, Artis Gilmore of Jacksonville.

"I can't believe there's a better sophomore in the country," said Minuteman coach Jack Leaman. "And if I'm right, most people just notice half of Julius' abilities, his scoring and rebounding. But he can also make the super pass like a Bob Cousy, can hit a man at three-quarters court when we fast break, and he plays outstanding defense, too. Let's face it, when a player his size is second nationally in rebounding, he has to be doing something right."

There were some honors after the season, such as New England Player of the Year, All-East Sophomore of the Year, and Honorable Mention All-American, but nothing higher than that. There was one chance for some additional recognition. For the first time in their history, the Minutemen were invited to play in the National Invitation Tournament at Madison Square Garden in New York City.

All of the University of Massachusetts players were exciting, especially Julius. The Garden is still the most prestigious arena in the country to many players. Now Julius and his teammates would join a field that included nationally ranked Marquette University, featuring all-American Dean Meminger, and Louisiana State University, with Pete Maravich, the nation's leading scorer.

Unfortunately, University of Massachusetts drew top-ranked Marquette as its first opponent. The team played hard and Julius was outstanding, but the Warriors had too much talent and depth. They won a hard-fought, 62–55, victory, eliminating the Minutemen from the tourney. It was to be Marquette's closest game of the competition, as they swept to the NIT title with Meminger the MVP. By playing them so close, Julius and his teammates had nothing to be ashamed about.

During the summer months in 1970, Julius was chosen to compete with the U.S. National Team in a series of exhibition games that would take them to Europe and the Soviet Union. He enjoyed it immensely, later saying:

"It was a once-in-a-lifetime opportunity, seeing the differences between the countries. We met people all over. Moscow wasn't a very friendly city and few people spoke English. But in Poland, Finland, and Estonia, the people went out of their way to talk with us, show us around, and make us feel very comfortable."

The Doctor enjoyed his stay with the National Team and then returned to Massachusetts for his junior year. Though he had been chosen to perform with some of the top players in the country, he continued to be a rather unknown and unheralded collegiate player. Most pre-season all-American projections omitted him entirely, and those who were questioned about it gave the standard answer. The Doctor played for a small school against second-rate competition, so he couldn't expect to be rated as highly as the major college stars.

"I knew I was as good as the guys getting all the recognition," Julius said, "so it didn't bother me that I wasn't considered an all-American. My main objective was to play well and help the team. As for the pros, I knew they didn't take only all-Americans. We had a strong team going into 1970-71 and it would have been interesting if we played a more independent schedule. But we had to stick with basically Yankee Conference teams. When I looked at our schedule, I figured we'd win 23 of our 26 games."

Sure enough, the Doctor was brilliant again in 1970-71, and he had a solid supporting cast. The club won many of its games by wide margins, and in every game, Julius would do something new, something that would dazzle the fans, the players, and the coaches. There seemed to be no limit to the innovative moves he would execute. Like any artist, he created on the basketball court, and though he was still largely unknown outside of New England, those who had followed his development continued comparing him to the so-called superstars.

The Doctor's play consistently bordered on the spectacular as the season entered its final stages. The University of Massachusetts was having a fine season, as predicted, and the team once again hoped for a post-season tournament bid. But that wasn't the Doctor's only consideration. He found himself facing an enormous decision, perhaps the biggest of his life.

Under traditional circumstances, Julius would not be eligible for pro ball until after the 1971-72 season, his senior year. Even if he were to leave school, pro teams wouldn't draft him until his original college class graduated. That rule had been observed by the pro football and basketball leagues for years, though technically it was more of a tradition, an *unwritten* rule. So then, what would be Julius' decision? He'd be back for his senior year and then turn pro if he'd so chose.

Well, things had been changing around this time. The young American Basketball Association was struggling for its very survival. The majority of graduating college stars still chose the more prestigious NBA, where there was more exposure, better competition, and more solvent franchises. In other words, the NBA wasn't about to fold.

In an attempt to get some one-upmanship on the older league, the ABA began drafting a few top undergraduates, enticing them to leave school before their class graduated and accept big pro contracts. Not to be outdone, the NBA didn't wait long before adopting the process also. Both leagues explained their new policies by claiming they took only those undergrads whose families needed the financial aid immediately. The ABA called it "special circumstance" and the NBA's term was "hardship," and its a practice that continues to this day. Strangely enough, the special circumstance or hardship cases always seemed to be star players who would be near the top of a team's draft list anyway.

Though Julius didn't have the visibility of many

other college stars, the pro scouts weren't about to miss a talent like his. So in the final few months of his junior season at the University of Massachusetts, he began getting feelers from a number of pro teams. Knowing the Doctor of a few years earlier, the guess would have been that he'd have given them a quick no, opting to finish college first. But things had been changing for him.

"When I went to college, my priorities were school first, basketball second, and the other stuff third," he said. "But the priorities slowly began shifting. I felt I was a more complete player as a junior. I was developing rapidly and that's when I started to think seriously about playing in the pros. So when people began contacting me I had to admit that basketball now meant more than anything else and I'd have to give signing some serious consideration."

So there was considerable pressure on the Doctor during the latter part of the 1970-71 season, but he didn't let it affect his play or his relationship with his teammates. The Minutemen swept the Yankee Conference title with a 23-3 record for the season, exactly as Julius had predicted before it all started, and for the second straight year, the team was invited to compete in the National Invitation Tournament.

Once again the Minutemen hoped for national recognition by showing well in the tourney, and once again they were disappointed. Unlike the previous year, when they played eventual winner Marquette real tough, they had a horrid game and were blown out by tough North Carolina, 90-49. It was of little consolation that the Tar Heels would go on to win the tourney. Neither Julius nor his teammates had played well. They were embarrassed by their showing, a disheartening finish to what had been a great year.

In spite of the NIT defeat, the Doctor had put together another brilliant season. He averaged 26.9 points a game, 12th best in the entire country, and once again he was a demon on the boards, grabbing 19.5 rebounds per contest. That was third best in the nation, behind Artis Gilmore of Jacksonville, the only man to top him the year before, and 6-8 Kermit Washington of American University. Of course, the stats were more or less academic. The big question was whether Julius would be back at the University of Massachusetts for his senior year or would he turn pro?

His coach, Jack Leaman, was more or less resigned to losing his star and harbored no bitterness. In fact, he pretty much gave the Doctor his blessing.

"We couldn't stand in his way," Leaman said. "It just wouldn't be fair to Julius for us to try to hold him back. After all, we had been boasting about his basketball ability for two years. So if he goes pro he'll just prove that everything we were saying about him was true."

And the Doctor himself didn't keep it a secret for long in which direction his mind was running.

"I'm ready to be thrown into the deep water," he said, "and I think I'm ready to swim."

The ABA, in those days, didn't always stick to strict drafting procedures. To get the top players, they'd do almost anything, including pretty much letting the player pick his team in some circumstances, or placing him where he would have the greatest impact on the fans. With the Doctor, the first choice was a natural.

When the ABA first started, the closest thing to a New York franchise was the New Jersey Americans. The Americans played out of Teaneck, New Jersey, at the old Teaneck Armory, and were never successful in drawing fans from the surrounding area. Finally, the team was moved to Long Island, where they would play out of the newly-constructed Nassau Coliseum, located in Uniondale, just a stone's throw from East Meadow, where the Doctor was born.

It came as no surprise when the Doctor said his first choice would be the Nets. He would, in effect, be playing right in his own backyard. It seemed like the perfect marriage. Then, much to his dismay, Julius learned the Nets weren't interested. It wasn't because they didn't recognize his talent. Rather, the Nets' Coach and General Manager, Lou Carnesecca, had his own reasons for turning down a chance to acquire the Doctor.

"My feelings were that if we kept raiding the colleges," Carnesecca said, "we'd lose the free farm system they provide. But I guess if I knew how things would be in the following years, I'd have signed him."

With the door to the Nets closed, Julius' agents went back to work. They began talking with another ABA team, the Virginia Squires. It didn't take long for a deal to be worked out and Julius announced he'd be leaving the University of Massachusetts to play with the ABA Squires on a four-year deal worth some $500,000.

He'd be joining a Virginia team that by ABA standards was quite good. In fact, the year before Julius' arrival, the Squires compiled a 55–29 regular season mark, the best in the league. Though they were upset in the playoffs by Kentucky, the

Squires were considered one of the top teams in the still-young league.

The club already had a bona fide superstar. He was Charlie Scott, a thin, but lightning-fast 6 ft 6 in. guard out of North Carolina. Scott was a bona fide all-American for the Tar Heels and was one of a growing number of top collegians beginning to choose the ABA over the NBA. The year Julius came in there was another prize catch, 7 ft. 2 in. center Artis Gilmore of Jacksonville, who passed up the NBA to join the Kentucky Colonels of the younger league.

It didn't take the Doctor long to test his wings as a pro. Remember, the colleges at that time had the no-dunk rule and Julius could exhibit his great variety of stuff only in practice. So once a pro, it was open season on slam-dunks. The first exhibition game was against the Colonels and Gilmore. Three times during the contest, the Doctor went to the hoop on the big guy with incredible moves, ending each with rim-shaking stuff. And in the ensuing games, he was going to the hoop every chance he had, still finding time for some outside shooting and a lot of rebounding. But it was his dunking that really turned the fans on, and the Doctor explained why.

"The no dunking rule came in my senior year in high school, so I hadn't been allowed to slam in competition for four years. So when I first started playing with the Squires I couldn't get enough of it. Once I got it out of my system I went back to shooting simple lay-ups most of the time.

"Of course, when I felt our team needed a big dunk as a psychological lift, then I'd slam. It gets the crowd up, our team up, and me up. Because of the excitement, we'll often start to defend better, play better all around."

Before that first exhibition season ended, the Doctor already had scores of people singing his praises, many of them after seeing him only once. For instance, veteran NBA-ABA referee, Earl Strom, said this:

"I've been around a long time and I've seen a lot of ballplayers come and go, but I've never seen one like Julius. I knew it after working just one exhibition game. He showed me moves I've never seen experienced men make, much less a rookie."

Veteran forward Doug Moe was a teammate of Julius with the Squires that year and he put it this way:

"The first time I saw him warm up I thought, 'Oh, no, here we go again, another showboat!' Boy, was I wrong. Julius was the most mature rookie I've ever seen. He comes at you with those long, open strides, and you have a tendency to keep backing away from him because you think he's not really making his move yet. But that's a mistake, because if you don't go up and challenge him, he'll simply glide right past you."

They weren't the only ones. John Kerr, the Squires Vice President and a former NBA center, said, "You can use all the adjectives in the book to describe some of Julius' moves and you still can't come close to describing how great he is."

One of the Doctor's biggest boosters was his new coach with Virginia, Al Bianchi, himself an NBA guard for some dozen seasons. Bianchi recalls the first time he laid eyes on the Doctor.

"When he first walked into the room my first impression was that he might be too thin," Bianchi said. "Then I caught sight of his hands. I just couldn't believe them. I suddenly wasn't so worried about him being thin.

"Now I feel that with a little more experience Julius will be the best forward to ever have played the game, the absolute best. The only one I can compare to Julius is Elgin Baylor. Both have great body control. Julius can put the ball down as well as Baylor, he can shoot as well, can run better, can rebound better and play defense a heck of a lot better. Plus, he can shoot with either hand."

That was quite a compliment, considering that most experts consider Baylor one of the two or three greatest forwards ever. But once he joined the Squires, Julius never took a backward step, never disappointed, just seemed to get better and better, more dazzling and confident with each passing game.

Five games into the regular season, the Doctor was averaging 23 points and 17 rebounds a game. He certainly wasn't afraid to mix it up underneath with bigger, stronger men, and although Charlie Scott was the team's leading scorer, Julius was right behind in a strong supporting role. In fact, after playing a patterned, disciplined game in college, the Doctor was glad to run into a player like Scott.

"Charlie was a great freelance player," Julius said. "He worked very hard for his openings and shots. Since I thought of myself as the same type of player I knew I could do things with the ball once I got it. The two of us combined to give the Squires quite an offense that year."

The Squires had more young players than the previous season and consequently made mistakes.

They were still a winning team, but not an overpowering one. That distinction went to Kentucky, which had the towering Gilmore at center. The Colonels were the class of the league during the regular season, but the Doctor was still the guy who drew the most raves.

With the Kentucky team making a complete shambles of the Eastern Division race, Virginia knew long before the season ended that it was destined for second place at best. The team continued to play over .500, but not at the pace they had set the season before. Then, with just 11 games remaining in the regular season, the team received a stunning blow.

It was learned that Charlie Scott had jumped the Squires and signed a contract with the Phoenix Suns of the NBA. No one could know it then, but it was the beginning of a pattern that would spell the eventual demise of the young league. But for now, it left the club without its quarterback and the league's leading scorer, since Scott was hitting at a 34.5 clip when he left.

Now the Doctor was on the spot more than ever. He was suddenly the main man, called upon to fill the void left by Scott's defection. He had to be the big scorer and floor leader. It was a tremendous burden to place on the shoulders of a 21-year-old rookie, but the Doctor responded without a second thought.

He asserted himself more than ever in the team's final 11 games, getting them ready for the playoffs. When the season ended, the Squires were in second place with a 45-39 record, miles behind the Colonels, which had one of the best records in pro basketball history, 68-16.

What a rookie year it had been for the Doctor. Playing in all 84 regular-season games, he scored 2,290 points, good for a 27.3 average, sixth best in the league. He shot 50 percent from the field and 75 percent from the foul line. He also grabbed 1,319 rebounds, a 15.7 average and third best in the ABA. Ironically, he was not named the league's Rookie of the Year. That distinction went to his old rival, Artis Gilmore, who helped the Kentucky team to its marvelous record.

In the playoffs that year, however, Julius showed the world that he indeed might really be the rookie of the century, the league voters notwithstanding. The opening round pitted the Squires against a team called the Miami Floridians, long since disbanded. The Squires won it in four straight, as the Doctor controlled the game, scoring and rebounding, and making plays. In fact, he set an ABA record in game three by tossing in 53 big points.

After the sweep, the Squires awaited the winner of the Kentucky-New York series, fully expecting to meet the powerhouse Colonels. But the Nets pulled a miraculous upset in six games and were still relishing their victory when they traveled to Virginia. The Squires won the first two games easily and seemed well on their way to the finals. But the Nets re-grouped, tied the series in New York, and led by forward Rick Barry and guard John Roche, won the series in seven games.

So the Squires were finished for the year, but nonetheless, Julius had been amazing throughout the playoffs. In 11 games he scored 366 points for a 33.2 average and also grabbed 224 rebounds, an incredible 20.2 per game. His playoff performance far exceeded his season's output, the first evidence of his rising to the occasion, something he would continue to do throughout his pro career.

Shortly after it ended, the Doctor had a chance to reflect and talk about the things he observed and learned during his rookie year as a pro.

"I wasn't a good shooter when I first went to college," he said, "so I always practiced, both before and after games, something which has carried over to this past season. Despite playing inside mostly early in the year, I kept practicing the outside shooting and it really paid off when Charlie Scott left the team. I handled the ball more often then and found myself having to shoot from the outside.

"Another thing in college was that I often just outjumped everyone. You might say I did my thing in the kitchen and got out. But in the pros, I found there was a lot more shoving and bumping, and they often got away with it, and there was also a lot more holding. So when I had the ball I found myself getting held, grabbed, kicked, you name it. And defensively, I was playing as I had in college and getting beat.

"But I learned. I found I could simply outrun some of the guys that held, so I began using my speed to the fullest advantage. Other times, I just rolled with the punches. It took awhile to accustom myself to pro defense and also how to protect myself on offense. You have to learn these things or you'll wind up with an injury."

There was no longer any doubt about the Doctor's ability. His future in pro ball seemed secure, barring injury, of course, but before the 1972–73 season started, the question was not how well he'd play, but just where he'd play. It seems as if the Doctor was unhappy about the way the Squires were administering his contract.

First of all, he said he hadn't received any bonus money, and a good deal of his $500,000 contract was in deferred payments, meaning it would be paid to him later over a long period of time. While the money had been personally guaranteed him, according to Julius, he began worrying when he learned that the Squires were having financial problems as a team. Pretty soon, a wide rift was developing between Julius and the owners of the team.

"I was pretty much broke before I started playing with Virginia," Julius said. "I didn't even have any money to live on and when I asked the team to rework my contract so I could get some money, they denied ever giving me any guarantees."

The situation worsened when Julius began hearing stories that Scott had jumped the team because of similar reasons, failing to receive money allegedly promised him. When the Squires refused to make any changes in the agreement, Julius made a bold move. He signed a three-year contract with the Atlanta Hawks of the NBA, a pact which gave him a bonus of $250,000 that he was to keep whether or not he ever played for them, and a balance of $1,800,000 along with an apartment or a car.

"I didn't really want to jump the Squires," Julius said, "but I wasn't sure they'd be able to fulfill their agreements."

Soon, the whole thing was turning into quite a mess. It seemed the Hawks didn't own the NBA rights to the Doctor. The Milwaukee Bucks had originally drafted him the previous spring, so NBA Commissioner J. Walker Kennedy said he could not play for Atlanta. At the same time, the Squires went to court to force the Doctor to complete his contractual obligations to them.

All this was happening as the 1972–73 season was about to begin. In fact, Julius played a couple of pre-season games with the Hawks before he was ordered to stop, and as usual he was exciting and impressive.

"Erving's moves are beautiful and they don't disrupt the team," said veteran Hawk forward Jim Washington. "He utilizes most of his moves on fast breaks or semi-fast breaks, so they're not out of context."

Finally, the courts made a ruling. Julius would have to return to the ABA and play for the Squires once again. The ABA season was already four-games old, but Julius returned and said he completely accepted the decision.

"I've got to play ball for Virginia and that's what I'm going to do," he said. "I'll worry about the future later."

Julius returned and was treated like anything but a deserter. The Squires played their home games at three sites, Norfolk, Hampton, and Richmond, and in each place he received a standing ovation. With the Doctor back in the lineup, the Squires quickly won four straight games, and before long, he was atop the league in scoring.

"There was never any question that I wanted Julius back or how well he would play once he returned," said Coach Al Bianchi. "That's just the kind of guy he is. And as soon as he got back he began making personal appearances again. All we have to do is ask. In a lot of ways, we owe him more than he owes us."

Despite the Doctor's presence, the Squires were no longer a powerhouse. The financially troubled franchise had dealt away the higher priced veterans and were going with kids. "The year before I was a rookie, but the second year I felt like an old timer on the Squires compared to the other guys," was the way the Doctor put it.

The Squires were .500 team that year, finishing dead even at 42–42, though the Doctor won his first ABA scoring title with 2,268 points in 71 games for a 31.9 average. In the playoffs, the team lost in the first round to Kentucky, four games to one, as the Doctor averaged 29.6, but he just didn't have the supporting cast to take the team any further.

Though Julius didn't know it then, his whole future course as a pro was about to be changed. The Squires were still having bad financial problems, and as had been their pattern in the past, they looked to make up some of the deficit by dealing away their star, and this time it was Julius. In fact, the entire league was worried about the deal. The ABA was still on shaky ground and they didn't want to lose the Doctor to the rival NBA.

The most logical move seemed to be bringing Julius home to New York. The Nets were playing in the brand new Nassau Coliseum and there's an old axiom saying that every league needs a strong franchise in New York to survive. Negotiations began between the Squires and New York Nets. On August 1, 1973, it was announced that Julius Erving was being sold to the Nets. The Doctor was home.

It was a complex, seven-year deal that would bring Julius some $1.9 million when it was completed, and he signed it happily. The Nets reportedly gave the Squires $750,000 for the Doctor, and also had to pay the Atlanta Hawks another $400,000 or so, settling the contract that the Doctor had signed with them.

"I feel this is going to be a great experience for me and the team," an exuberant Julius proclaimed. "I can do the things that will help us win, and the other guys feel it, too. That's just as important."

There was a great deal of excitement surrounding the 1973-74 Nets team. Lou Carnesecca had returned to college coaching at St. John's, and the new coach was another New Yorker, Kevin Loughery, who had starred at St. John's, then had been a standout back-courtman in the NBA. For a short time, he had also coached the Philadelphia 76'ers of the NBA. He, too, was happy to be home.

Aside from the Doctor, the team had another potentially fine forward in 6 ft. 9 in. rookie Larry Kenon. The center was 6 ft. 11 in. Billy Paultz, another native New Yorker; and the guards were speedy Brian Taylor and veteran John Roche. Billy Melchionni and rookie John Williamson gave the club depth on the backline. Billy Schaeffer and Willie Sojourner would help up front and the entire team averaged just 22.6 years of age, making the Nets one of the youngest teams in basketball.

It was because of their youth that most basketball writers predicted the Nets would finish third in the Eastern Division, behind Kentucky and Carolina, and many thought they detected a pattern when the Doctor scored 42 points in the season opener, yet the team lost to the Indiana Pacers, 118-99.

They hadn't even come close, showing little balance or cohesion, with numerous holes in the defense.

"The guys have to learn to work together," Loughery said. "They're all young and eager to learn, so I don't expect it will be long before we start rolling."

In the following week, Loughery began looking like a prophet. With the Doctor leading the way, the team won four straight games, whipping Virginia, Carolina, Memphis, and Utah. Suddenly the club was leading the division with a 4-1 mark and did, indeed, seem to be on its way. But sometimes, when things look the brightest, they begin to go sour.

Suddenly, the club began losing, the excitement of the four-game winning streak was forgotten and the realities of such a young club became evident.

From a 4-1 start, the team lost nine straight and plummeted to 4-10. Fortunately, team president Roy Boe voiced confidence in his rookie coach and allowed him time to get a grasp on the situation, and Loughery slowly did just that. Julius, of course, had been playing very well despite the losses, but Loughery soon saw that there was a subtle psychological drawback to having a player like Julius on the team.

"You get a guy like Doc and you begin to feel you're supposed to win," the coach said. "I think some of the guys might have felt that all we needed to do was relax and watch Doc operate. I might have been getting a bit like that myself before I realized that other changes had to be made."

First of all, the coach saw he had to change his own style, his approach to the team.

"I had always been an emotional player," he said, "and I thought it would be good to keep my team at an emotional pitch. So I was doing a lot of yelling and screaming for their benefit. Soon, I realized that approach was passé, that the youth of my players didn't faze them, so it shouldn't faze me. Despite their youth, they were so confident it was almost scary. Screaming at them was the wrong approach, so I corrected it."

Loughery also changed the team's defensive style, stressing the concept of team defense, but abandoning the early-season tactic of pressing all over the floor. That had only served to disorganize the club. He also decided to insert rookie guard John Williamson into the starting lineup and use veteran Billy Melchionni off the bench. This move helped, too, because it gave Williamson more confidence and the club needed his physical strength on the floor, and it enabled Melchionni to be a steadying influence off the bench when things began to go sour.

Once again, the team began winning, and before long they were again challenging Kentucky and Carolina for divisional supremacy. As for Julius, he was still performing miracles. Once again, his stats were imposing. He was locked in a battle with Kentucky's Dan Issel for the scoring lead. In addition, he was in the top ten in rebounding, and in the top five in blocked shots and steals. There wasn't anything he couldn't do on the floor.

When the going got tough late in the game, that's when the Doctor would really take charge. In a low-scoring game against Kentucky, the Nets trailed by a 68–60 count with just nine minutes left. Loughery called a timeout, told the team to press on defense, and get the ball to the Doctor on offense.

"The way it was going, I told Doc he'd have to pull this one out for us. It was amazing how he took over, doing everything at both ends."

He began scoring on an assortment of drives, jumpers, and dunks, scoring 16 of the club's final 23 points. He also got what proved to be the game-winner, then went down to the other end and blocked a last-second shot by 7-2 Artis Gilmore to preserve an 83–82 win. The Doctor ended up with 30 points, and what's more, he and the Nets were proving they were for real.

By this time, Julius was beginning to completely understand his role in the club. "When I learned I was coming here I knew I'd have to be a leader," he said. "Bill Melchionni is our captain, and in effect, our designated leader, which is the way it should be. I try to lead in a different way. For instance, before I came here the Nets had a reputation of squabbling among themselves when they were losing. Sure, there has to be some criticism among players on a team, but I try to steer it in a positive direction, cut down on the meaningless kind of griping. For instance, you shouldn't blame a guy for missing a pass. Instead, you've got to boost him up by saying you'll connect on it next time. So I guess I'm trying to be a moderating and unifying force."

Whatever the formula, it was working for all the Nets. By the All-Star Game break, the Nets had moved into first place with a 34–20 record, compared to a 31–19 slate for Kentucky. And in the team's final game before the break, the Doctor had tossed in 46 against Carolina to take over the scoring lead from Dan Issel by a slim margin. In addition, the team had strengthened itself through a trade with Kentucky, bringing tough forward Wendell Ladner and defensive guard Mike Gale to the Nets for shooting guard John Roche. The club was now ready for the second half.

The Doctor also made a deal of his own about that time. He married a girl named Turquoise Brown, whom he had met while still playing for the Squires. It was turning into a great season for him in every way.

And as the season wore down, the Nets continued to battle the Colonels for the top spot in the East. In a big game against the Colonels in Lexington, the Doctor was absolutely brilliant. He was virtually unstoppable all through the game, yet it went into overtime. With the score tied and just seconds left, he got the ball and went one-on-one against defensive forward Ron Thomas. The Doctor maneuvered inside the key, turned and took a 15-footer—*SWISH*—success!

The shot gave the Nets a 114–112 victory, and the Doc had scored 41 points, including 11 of the Nets 13 in the overtime. Afterward, an exuberant Doctor said this:

"I loved being able to finish the game like that. In fact, it's the part of the game I really loved as a kid, the challenge of daring to be great!"

Julius and his teammates continued to respond to Loughery's coaching, and when the season ended, they were in first place with a 55–29 mark, two games ahead of Kentucky. Even more impressive was their 51–19 mark from the lowpoint of 4–10 early in the year.

Individually, the Doctor had another great season. He took his second straight scoring title with 2,299 points in 84 games, good for a 27.4 average, enabling him to beat out Indiana forward George McGinnis. A short time later, he was named the ABA's Most Valuable Player. And the Doctor explained how he continued to work on his game, even with his great success.

"The majority of my moves are instinctive," he said, "but I can do these things because I still put in the time experimenting with them, developing and polishing new things. Therefore, I know what I can do in various kinds of situations. So when a situation arises, I don't have to think about it. I just go. It's a court awareness, a complete knowledge of the situation and what to do when it occurs. And you can't be inhibited in your thoughts or actions."

In the opening round of the playoffs, the Nets eliminated Virginia easily in five games, setting up an Eastern showdown with Kentucky, which had beaten Carolina in four straight games. Everyone expected it to be a hard-fought battle, but it turned out to be anything but. The Nets won it in four straight games, winning three easily, and the other by two points. They were looking like a powerhouse.

The final round saw the Nets going up against the Utah Stars. Once again Julius and his teammates did their thing. With the Doctor tossing in 47, the Nets won the opener, 89–85. Game two saw Julius score 32 as the Nets rambled to a 61–37 halftime lead and coasted home with a 118–94 win. They were getting closer to that title.

Game three was a real team effort, the Nets coming from behind, making up three points in the final ten seconds, then winning in overtime, 103–100. Now the New Yorkers needed just one more. Utah stalled the celebration by winning the fourth game, 97–89, but in game five they put it together again. Julius had 20 points, rookie Kenon had 23, and another rookie, John Williamson had 15 as the Nets won the Championship, 111–100.

Once again, the Doctor led the way with a 27.9 average for 14 playoff games and was named MVP. So the Nets were a big, happy family. Guard Brian Taylor said, "We'll be back here again. This team has the ability to win a lot of championships. And Doc's the guy who'll do it for us."

Coach Loughery also had high praise for his superstar. "He's far and away the greatest player I've ever been around," said the coach, "and he's a lot more than that, too. He's also one of the greatest people I've ever been around, just a super guy."

Taking in the basic facts, it would seem the young Nets were on the brink of a dynasty. But there were underlying problems that at this point had nothing to do with the team. Even though they were champs, the Nets were not drawing the fans to the Nassau Coliseum. The Islanders hockey team, who also played at the Coliseum far outdrew the Nets and had much less success. So in spite of the title, the team was losing money at the gate.

Many people tried to guess why the Nets, with an exciting young team and the most electrifying player in the game, weren't drawing. One of the common conclusions wasn't a pretty one. Unlike most sports arenas, which are located in the heart of large cities, the Nassau Coliseum was in the midst of mainly suburban Long Island. It was felt that area fans did not care to see the Nets or the visiting teams because basketball had become a predominantly black sport, while hockey was all white. That might not have been the only reason, but there had to be some truth in it.

That wasn't all. The ABA itself was in financial trouble. The teams had paid out small fortunes to the big stars in a bidding war with the NBA, which was draining on the cash registers. Now, many of those stars were jumping to the established NBA, anticipating the demise of the ABA, which was the prevailing rumor more often than not.

By 1974-75, Julius Erving had become *the* big drawing card in the ABA. Wherever the Nets went, the fans came out to see the team and the fabulous Doctor, yet the team still wasn't drawing well at home. And that's when many writers and observers began saying that Julius was the least known and least seen great athlete in America. Outside of the ABA towns, not that many people knew how great Doc was.

The Nets were winning again in 1974-75, and were in another dog-fight with Kentucky for the East title. That made them even more attractive to the dwindling numbers of ABA fans. As one writer put it:

"By the end of 1973-74, the Nets were so dominant that they not only won the league title, but became like a barnstorming team on tour of a struggling circuit, bringing in almost 1,500 extra fans wherever they went. This season has seen similar results."

But the ABA was also without a national TV contract, and without that money and exposure, the consensus was that the league couldn't last much longer. Playing under this kind of cloud, the

Nets finished 1974–75 with a 58–26 mark, tying Kentucky for the division title. The Colonels then won it in a one-game playoff.

The Doctor had another fine season, averaging 27.8 points, though he failed to take a third straight scoring title. Yet he and his teammates hoped to repeat as league champs. Their first-round opponent would be a team called the Spirit of St. Louis, a loosely-disciplined outfit that could score, but didn't play much defense. The Nets were overwhelming favorites.

They won the first game and seemed to be on their way. Then, without warning, the club went completely flat. The St. Louis team caught fire and sensing the Nets vulnerability, swept the next four games in a gigantic upset. So it was over. The club wouldn't repeat, though the Doctor repeated his league's Most Valuable Player award for the second straight year.

Because of the poor playoff showing, team officials decided to make changes. They surprised everyone by trading center Billy Paultz, forward Larry Kenon, and guard Mike Gale to San Antonio for forward Rich Jones, centers Swen Nater and Kim Hughes, and forward Chuck Terry.

The Nets played well, the new players seeming to blend in, and the Doctor still doing his aerial act. But the ABA wasn't flying in 1975–76. On the contrary, it was folding, its demise now seemed inevitable. Several more teams disbanded during the year and the remaining clubs were condensed into a single, six-team circuit. Most of the stars were gone, the league's other top forward, George McGinnis of Indiana, having jumped to Philadelphia of the NBA. In truth, during the second half of the year, the ABA hardly resembled a professional sports league at all.

None of that deterred Julius. He never complained about the situation and continued to play his own, unique brand of basketball. As one writer said, "some players have been called 'the franchise,' but Julius Erving has become 'the league.' " And it was true, he was the only player left who could draw a crowd. The fans sensed it was a last hurrah for the league, and not knowing if their cities would have teams the next year, they wanted to see the Doctor one more time.

The Nets finished the season with a 55-29 record, second to Denver in the six-team loop. Julius regained the scoring title with 2,462 points in 84 games for a 29.3 average. He would also be named league MVP for the third straight time. Now came what could very well be the last ABA playoffs.

San Antonio was the first round opponent for the Nets, and the series was a fine one, going the full seven games. The New Yorkers finally pulled it out, 121-114, with Julius again playing outstanding ball. That put the Nets in the final against Denver, considered the league's best team, a club led by veteran center Dan Issel, forward Bobby Jones, and a super-rookie named David Thompson.

The challenge of the big series brought out the best in the Doctor. In game one he tossed in 45 points as the Nets won a squeaker, 120-118. He was even better the second time, getting 49, only this time Denver won, 127-121. Still, more than ever the Nets were the Doctor's team, and he had the green light to do whatever he wanted on the court. Though his aim was always a winning effort with the team coming first, he nevertheless showed those lucky enough to see it, the full repertoire of his talent.

Still playing inspired ball, he led his team to victory in the next two games, 117–111, and 121–112. Denver rallied to win game five, 118–110, but in game six the Nets won their second championship, 112–106, and as it turned out, the last title in the American Basketball Association.

Julius had averaged 34.6 points in 13 playoff games and grabbed 164 rebounds. Naturally, he was the playoff MVP and had shown once again what an immense talent he had become.

Then, shortly after it all ended, the word came out. The ABA was folding, but the NBA had decided to take four of the franchises into the older league. So in 1976–77, the Nets, Denver, San Antonio, and Indiana would move to the NBA. The other two teams would disperse and their players drafted around the league. Finally, the Doctor would be given the exposure he deserved, and his fans couldn't wait for him to lead the Nets into the NBA.

During the offseason, the team made another big trade, sending guard Brian Taylor to Kansas City in return for all-star guard Nate "Tiny" Archibald. Archibald was considered one of the game's best, a penetrating guard who picked up assists by the bushel. The thought of Tiny teaming with the Doctor made Nets' fans drool.

But before the training camp opened, the Nets received some stunning news. The Doctor asked to have his contract, which still had four years to run, renegotiated. The Nets said they wouldn't do it, and suddenly, battle lines were drawn, and for the

Doctor this was serious.

His base salary for 1976 would be something over $225,000, but he was also aware that the newly-acquired Archibald was earning some $450,000 a year. In addition, he had learned that there were some 25 players in the NBA earning more than he was. That can eat at a player's pride, and it was coupled with the fact that he claimed the Nets had made a number of promises that weren't kept.

"I'm giving a lot of myself in every game," Julius said, "and I expect that when I'm told something, it will come to pass. I want to be in an atmosphere of trust and good faith. Until now, I have heard promises that weren't kept. I'm going to wait now until they are, and I want them in writing.

"I also know that I'm being exploited by just about all the teams in pro basketball, especially the Nets, and by TV. So I want to get this straightened out before we go into this season."

There was some truth to that. All the NBA teams were already promoting the first appearances by the Doctor in their cities, and much of the national TV schedule was being built around him. Still, some people thought he was being selfish. His Nets salary was a high one, no one would argue that, and he had signed a long-term contract. But Julius still felt the Nets should want to pay him his worth.

"The market today dictates that I should be paid more," he said.

Nets president Roy Boe was just as adamant. And the word was that he already had financial problems, so he couldn't really afford to double the Doctor's salary. Then when Julius said he wouldn't report without a new pact, Boe tried to keep the mood pleasant.

"Let there be no mistake about it," he said. "Julius Erving is one of the finest athletes and one of the finest persons in America's sports history... The Nets organization and their fans here in New York, as well as in all the NBA cities, greatly regret, and in time Julius will regret, his decision."

Julius kept his word and didn't report. He also sat out the exhibition season as the Nets struggled without him. But Boe was just as stubborn. He continued to refuse any renegotiation, and as the season approached, word filtered out of New York that Boe was trying to deal his reluctant superstar. So the tension was mounting. It was difficult to imagine the Doctor operating outside of New York, but it was also beginning to look as if there were no other way.

Then it happened. Just one day before the season opened, it was announced that Julius had been sold to the Philadelphia 76ers, and he had signed a six-year pact with Philly, estimated to be worth some $3.5 million.

The sports world was stunned. No one figured on Philadelphia, the once-proud franchise that had come down from Syracuse (where they were known as the Syracuse Nationals) and had once boasted the likes of Wilt Chamberlain, Billy Cunningham, and other stars. In 1966–67 the club had a regular season mark of 68–13 and went on to win the NBA title. But soon after Chamberlain and some other stars left and the franchise fell onto hard times.

By 1972–73 they were the laughing stock of the league, checking in with an ignominious 9–73 record. After that, they slowly began rebuilding, and when they got a new owner, Eugene "Fitz" Dixon, the rebuilding began in earnest. In 1975-76 they had signed 6 ft. 8 in. forward George McGinnis, the Doctor's old rival from the ABA. McGinnis became an all-star and the team leader, and with some other fine players like guard Doug Collins, forward Steve Mix, and guard Lloyd Free, they began winning, finishing with a 46-36 record for the year.

Now the Doctor was coming over. The first question was how would he fit in, and could he and McGinnis both share the same basketball and accept their roles on the team? But in the excitement of the transaction, no one was complaining.

"I'm just so excited," said Doug Collins. "I just can't imagine playing on the same team with George and Julius. The thought of what we could create on the court is beyond my imagination."

"When I heard Doc was coming I just fell down on my knees and cried," said 7 ft. center Caldwell Jones, who had also joined the team from the ABA. "At least I don't have to worry about him going to the hoop on me anymore."

McGinnis, too, seemed pleased and excited. "Some of the guys don't even know him," George said. "They've seen some clips of his dunks on TV and asked me if he can really do that stuff in a game. I told them they ain't seen nothing yet. I've seen him do that number over Artis Gilmore and he's 7'-2". I'll tell you, there's gonna be a lot of guys in this league standing around watching him when he gets started."

Though in his heart he didn't want to leave New York, Julius seemed quite pleased that he was going to Philly.

"This is going to be a good situation for me," he said. "I see potential here. Give us some time and we won't be losing many ballgames.

"I haven't played in competition for months so it'll take time for me. In my mind, I feel I can do anything I want on the court. But I don't think my body can do what my mind wants it to do yet. But my body will tell me when it's ready."

So without practicing with the team, Julius joined the Sixers for their opener against the Spurs. He had worn the number 32 through high school and college, but the Sixers had retired that number because it belonged to Billy Cunningham. Without complaint, Julius switched over to number 6, and that night he was announced before a packed house of more than 17,000 fans in the Philadelphia Spectrum. He received a two-minute standing ovation from the fans. He was officially a Sixer.

Julius didn't start, of course, but with five minutes and 51 seconds left in the first half, Coach Gene Shue sent him in. He was nervous and unsure at first. His first pass was stolen, and his first shot, a short jumper, was off. He also missed four free throws by halftime and didn't score.

But when he came back in near the end of the third period he was more relaxed. He hit on a layup near the end of the session for his first NBA points, and then played very well in the fourth period, scoring another 15 points. He wound up with 17 points in 16 minutes, but the Sixers lost the game, 121–118. Still, his debut had been a good one and everyone seemed pleased. The Sixers were already odds-on favorites to win the NBA title.

During the next few weeks the Sixers started winning and Julius was in the starting lineup. He seemed to work well with McGinnis and the club soon jumped atop the Atlantic Division over archrival Boston. There was a difference in his game, however. He wasn't the same kind of take-charge player. His game was more controlled as he tried to fit in, thus it was less spectacular. There were fewer one-on-ones, fewer slam dunks, and when pressed, Julius talked about his role.

"I can score 30 points any night," he said, "but that's not what this team needs from me. I'm not supposed to score thirty. We'd be in trouble if I did. I want to draw two men, want to make passes, want to take advantage of my strengths and George's. And I'd just like to make one good play that I can remember each game."

The team didn't pull away, however. Soon they began losing games they should have won, and on more than one occasion they were actually blown out by weaker teams. The formula wasn't really working. In mid February, Julius was chosen for the All-Star Game, starting for the East along with McGinnis at forward.

Suddenly the Doctor was dominating. He was all over the court, rebounding, scoring, dunking. At one point he went high in the air on the drive and slam-dunked the ball over 7 ft. 2 in. Kareem Abdul-Jabbar, the best center in the game. When it ended, the East lost by a point, but Julius had scored 30 and pulled down 12 rebounds. He was named the game's Most Valuable Player.

"I haven't played much like the Doctor this year," he admitted, afterward. "I've just been Julius Erving. But tonight I took the Doctor out of the closet. Maybe I'll keep him out awhile."

It was the first time Julius had even hinted that

he didn't like holding back in Philly, but he wouldn't come out and admit it directly. His biggest fan, his wife Turquoise, also saw the difference.

"I have seen Julius play every game this year, but this is the first time I've really seen him *play*," she said.

By late February, the Sixers were 34-20, but struggling, and more people were beginning to criticize the team and especially the way Julius was being used.

"I'll tell you," said one writer, "The 76ers have two of the best forwards in basketball, yet neither one of them gets the ball enough. They've got all that firepower up front and yet they are a guard-oriented team."

There certainly was a great deal of outside shooting from Collins, Free, and Henry Bibby. Coach Shue tried to characterize it all as a team concept and said that defenses always sag on Julius and McGinnis, necessitating the outside shooting. He claimed it was a different situation than the one in New York and that Julius just wasn't in a position to do the same things anymore. But Nets coach Kevin Loughery looked at it differently.

"It really hurts me to see Doc now," said Loughery. "He's not enjoying the game anymore. He doesn't have that bright look in his eye, and he's surely not doing the things he can do.

"The fans are the ones losing out as well, because they can no longer see the greatest show in basketball. It just isn't there, and it can't be in his present situation."

Many of these little subtleties were not readily apparent to the average fan. The players pretty much restrained themselves from popping off too much, and the Doctor didn't really complain at all. In fact, Julius is probably the most diplomatic and least complaining superstar in the sport. But his wife, Turquoise, in an interview in mid-March, expressed some feelings that might also have reflected the Doctor's thoughts.

"Julius and I miss New York," she said. "We would have preferred that the Nets not sell him to the Philadelphia 76ers last October, because New York is home ... The treatment in Philadelphia is not like the treatment we received from the Nets. It was like a family in New York, including Coach Kevin Loughery and his wife. We were one. In Philly, after a game, we go our own way."

She concluded by saying, "One thing would be nice, if the fans in Philly could really see Julius play. They haven't seen all of him yet. Julius is an unselfish team player. He would never say the things I say."

Most of the problems were forgotten when the Sixers checked in with a 50–32 record, winning the division by six games. Of the 22 NBA teams, only the Los Angeles Lakers had a better regular season mark, with Denver finishing with an identical slate as the Sixers. Experts still looked at the Doctor and McGinnis, and the supporting cast, and made the team odds-on favorite to win the playoffs.

In spite of his missing the preseason, Julius emerged as the Sixers leading scorer, playing in all 82 games and getting 1,770 points for a 21.6 average, but that was far off some of his ABA norms. McGinnis was right behind at 21.4, and Collins checked in at 18.3.

The Sixers drew a bye in the first round of the

playoffs, then had to go up against the Celtics in a best of seven games series. It was a hard-fought series, with the Celts taking the first game, but Philly came back to win four of the next five and advanced to the semi-finals against the Houston Rockets.

Philly won the first two games easily, but Houston came back in game three, and in that one the Sixers lost guard Lloyd Free with a rib injury. The fourth game was pivotal, and with Collins scoring 36 and the Doctor 29, the Sixers won it, 107–95, for a 3–1 lead.

The Rockets managed to win the fifth game, despite 37 points from the Doctor, but when Julius came back with 34 and Collins had 27 in the sixth game, Philly closed it out, 112–109. Now they were in the finals and would face the surprising Portland Trailblazers, led by center Bill Walton, forward Maurice Lucas, and guard Lionel Hollins.

It was obvious that the Doctor was taking charge more in the playoffs, though part of that was necessitated by a strange shooting slump that had befallen McGinnis. So the offense began revolving around the Doctor and Doug Collins. Still, the Sixers were favorites to take it all.

The one-two Sixer punch was in evidence in game one of the finals. Julius had 33 and Collins 30 as the team won, 107–101. When they came right back to win the second game, a 107–89 cakewalk, the Sixers were just two games from the title.

Now they were out in Portland and game three was very close for three quarters. Suddenly, the Blazers launched a devastating fastbreak as Walton began controlling the boards, and they ran away, 129–107, despite 28 more points by the Doctor. The game should have been a warning.

If it wasn't, the fourth game was. Portland was suddenly pointing up all the Philly weaknesses, the lack of team play, the standing around, the disorganization, and the cohesive Blazer team humiliated the Sixers, 130–98, again blasting it open in the second half. McGinnis' shooting slump was worse, Free was still hampered by the rib injury, and the Doctor and Collins couldn't do it alone.

Portland did it again in game five, 110–104. The Doctor had 37 in this one, but he just wasn't getting the help. Game six back in Portland was a close one, but the Blazers were poised and confident by now, and they won the NBA title, 109–107, sending Philly home as losers.

The Doctor had looked more like his old self in the playoffs, averaging 27.3 points for 19 playoff games. But coming away a loser didn't make him happy and he said to the fans of the Sixers, "We owe you one!"

Everyone hoped 1977–78 would be different, that movement and balance would be restored to the offense, and there would be more team defense. But there seemed to be griping from the beginning. Free, forward Joe Bryant, and 6 ft. 11 in., 250-pound kid center Darryl Dawkins all wanted more playing time. Dawkins had been signed right out of high school in 1975 and had a world of awesome potential. He felt he was ready to show it.

When the team lost four of its first six games, owner Fitz Dixon decided to move. He replaced Shue with Billy Cunningham, one of the Sixers' great stars of the past. But Cunningham had no previous coaching experience, and it was soon obvious that he'd be learning on the job.

There also seemed to be a change in McGinnis. There were some who felt the playoffs had pointed up the fact that Julius was now the unofficial leader of the team, and George's shooting slump against Portland alienated him from his teammates. Now, some people said, he wanted out, wanted to go somewhere where he could once again be the top gun. Cunningham first tried to smooth things over.

"I want everyone to feel he is contributing to the ballclub," he said. "I'm planning to make a few changes, like a faster-paced game, a little more pressure defense, running more, getting our centers involved in the offense. We are a family now and we have to keep our problems within, not let them get in the papers. I can be a player's friend and we can still talk, though I'm the one who will make the final decision."

Cunningham's presence seemed to bolster the team's morale at first. In late November they won four straight games, lost one to Washington, then reeled off ten more and seemed to be playing like a team at last. But, still, some of the small subtleties of the game were missing, and the non-starters were still reluctant to accept secondary roles with the club, as subs must do on any championship team.

Soon the complaints began, but through it all, the Doctor remained calm and didn't say much. He was not having a typical Erving year, averaging just over twenty points a game and there were even times when he found himself on the bench during crucial moments in the fourth period.

So he wasn't happy with the situation, either. In mid-March, it was said that Julius had a meeting with Cunningham and complained about not getting the ball down low, which was evident to most people, and for a while afterward, he began getting a chance to do more things inside. When he did, he was still unstoppable.

There was still no denying the raw talent. The team finished the year with a 55-27 mark, winning the division by a whopping 12 games. Only Portland had a better record in the league. The Doctor had his lowest scoring season ever, a 20.6 average, which led the team. Of course, if they could win in the playoffs, all would be forgotten.

But that wasn't going to happen. This time they made it to the Conference finals, only to be derailed by Washington in six games. The Doctor averaged 21.8 in ten playoff games, but it was now evident that changes would have to be made.

During the offseason they were. McGinnis was dealt to Denver for 6 ft. 9 in. forward Bobby Jones, a team and defensively oriented player who would be content to blend in and assume a role. The discontented Lloyd Free was sent to San Diego, and a rookie guard named Maurice Cheeks took his place.

It was a strange season for the Sixers in 1978-79. The team seemed to be working better on the whole with Julius, now the acknowledged leader, and more players, such as Jones and Cheeks, were able to accept set roles within the team. Cunningham seemed to be more confident in his coaches, yet the club didn't do as well as the year before. They finished behind Washington in the Atlantic Division with a 47-35 mark, and in the playoffs they were upset by the San Antonio Spurs in the conference semi-finals. It was beginning to look as if the Sixers would never win.

As for the Doctor, he had had his best year in the NBA, averaging 23.1 points in 78 games, 11th best in the league. And he seemed more content with Philly than ever before. Perhaps he felt the team was on the brink of putting it all together.

For the first time since the Doctor had arrived, no one was predicting big things. The 76ers came into 1979-80 as something of an unknown quantity. Would the team continue to backslide, or would they bounce back? It was evident from the start that it would be the latter.

Darryl Dawkins was now the starting center, and the big man was starting to produce. That left 7 ft. Caldwell Jones free to start at the forward position, where he could better utilize his quickness, and concentrate on defense and rebounding. Cheeks and Collins were the guards, with Cheeks the playmaker and Collins the shooter. Bobby Jones was the first forward off the bench, and he could play both the power and small forward positions. Behind him was the steady and reliable Steve Mix. Henry Bibby was a fine third guard and young Clint Richardson also contributed.

For the first time in years the Sixers had depth and players willing to accept their roles. They also had the Doctor looking as good as ever. In fact, for the first time in years Julius was playing without his knee braces, the result of some off-season conditioning. And he showed early on that when it was needed, he could produce the same kind of mind-boggling magic he had shown in his days with the Nets.

All season long the team battled the rejuvenated Boston Celtics for the division lead. The team was winning, but without the internal bickering of previous years. And everyone was contributing. Young Dawkins was proving especially awesome in the middle, and during the course of the season he actually shattered two backboards by the force of his slam dunks.

There was also new-found respect between players and their coach, as the Doctor mentioned late in the year.

"Billy has done a fantastic job," Julius said. "The guys have accepted him as a coach and their leader. In fact, I have never been part of a group of players more receptive to a coach. You can see it in the way they listen and absorb, and in our execution."

When Collins was injured in February, the team picked up guard Lionel Hollins from Portland and effectively filled the gap. And throughout the season the Doctor did more of the things he had done in the past. Now, the entire NBA fully appreciated his marvelous talents. At age 30, he still had his quickness, his marvelous ability to hang in the air and make his twisting, driving moves. And he still had those long strides that enabled him to take off from the foul line and slam the ball home.

At the season's end, the Sixers had a 59–23 record, finishing two games behind the Celtics, who were 61–21. But the team felt it was fully ready for the playoffs, and so did Julius. He had just completed his best NBA season ever, finishing fourth in the league in scoring with 2,100 points and a 26.9 average. But it was his overall contribution to the club that made him a first team all-star once again.

When the playoffs began it appeared as if the

76ers were approaching a peak. First they had to play Washington in a two of three mini-series. They swept that with no trouble, Julius scoring 31 in the second and clinching game. Now it was on to a best of seven with the always-scrappy Atlanta Hawks.

Many figured this one would go the full seven games and the first one was indeed close. Atlanta led by two at the half, and Philly by one after three. In the fourth period it was close again, but as was now the custom, the Doctor took over. He scored 11 of his 28 points in the final session, and threw a long pass to Bobby Jones for the clinching basket for a 107–104 victory.

"I was content to move the ball and get everyone involved," Doctor said. "But when the guys stopped hitting and it was the fourth quarter, then I wanted Billy to run some plays for me, and he did."

The Sixers were winners again in game two, but back in Atlanta the Hawks won, 105–93. This set up the pivotal fourth game. It was tied at the half at 46–all, but in the third period Philly broke it open, winning 107–83, with a balanced attack. So they held a 3–1 lead and returned to the Spectrum to try to wrap it up.

That they did, although Atlanta made it a battle. Julius had another great game with 30 points, including 10 of 10 from the foul line, but he had awesome support from young Dawkins, who also scored 30 and dominated underneath. The Sixers won, 105–100, and would now advance to the conference finals against archrival Boston, in what was expected to be a war.

The Celts had the best regular-season record in

the league and were led by a brilliant rookie, Larry Bird. But they had many other fine players, including center Dave Cowens, forwards Cedric Maxwell and M. L. Carr, and guards Tiny Archibald, Chris Ford, and Pete Maravich. As always, they played a fast-breaking team game, and would be extremely tough to beat.

The opener was close all the way, neither team able to break it open. Boston opened a 58-48 lead midway through the third period, but the Doctor scored ten points for Philly in a 16-2 spurt that gave them the lead.

As expected, it went down to the wire, Philly leading 94-93 with less than a minute left. Julius had the ball and drove underneath. When he was double-covered he slipped the ball back to Henry Bibby who hit a short jumper to put the icing on the cake. Philly held on to win, 96-93 on the Celts home court, as the Doctor scored 29 and Dawkins 23.

Boston reversed things in game two, winning 96-90, with rookie Bird getting 31, and in game three the series moved to Philly and the battle resumed. It was a two-point game at the half, but Philly broke it open in the third period. Julius became incensed when he was submarined by M. L. Carr and went on his own little scoring spree, hitting three straight to make the lead 90-76.

But the Celts scrambled back and made a game of it, their rally falling two points short as Philly won, 99-97, with the Doctor leading all scorers with 28. Game four was the easiest. Julius got 12 of his 30 points in the third period as Philly broke on top and won, 102-90, opening up a 3-1 lead. They were now primed for the upset.

The Sixers had momentum and wouldn't give it up. In game five they were awesome, winning 105-94, with everyone playing so well that Julius only had to score fourteen points. In fact, he took just ten shots, proving again he was an unselfish team player who did whatever it took to win. So once again the Sixers were on the brink of an NBA title. All they had to do now was defeat the Los Angeles Lakers.

No way would that be easy. The Lakers were a fine team, though perhaps lacking in depth. Kareem Abdul-Jabbar was still the best center in the league. He had good support from power forward Jim Chones, and small forward Jamaal Wilkes, coming off his best year. The starting backcourt was devastating, with speedy Norm Nixon and super rookie Earvin "Magic" Johnson, a 6 ft. 8 in. wizard who could handle the ball like a small man, rebound like a big man, and do anything else in between. The sixth man was Michael Cooper, a fine defensive player who could swing from forward to guard, as could Johnson. In the conference finals, the Lakers had easily defeated the defending champion Seattle Supersonics in five games.

Game one belonged to the Lakers and Kareem. The big center had 33 points and 14 rebounds as the Lakers pleased the home crowd with a 109–102 victory. Julius had just 20 and Dawkins fouled out after playing just eighteen minutes. Laker coach Paul Westhead said his team was really working to stop the Doctor.

"The key is to make him give the ball up outside. When you double-team, it puts pressure on him because he's such an unselfish player. He's not going to try to beat two guys from thirty feet by himself."

It was sweet revenge for Philly in game two. The Sixers took a 59-41 halftime lead, upped it to 89-71 at the end of three, and then had to hold off a furious Laker comeback to win, 107-104. Dawkins had 25 and Julius 23 in the winning effort, but the Laker comeback in the final period took some of the starch out of the victory.

Yet the Sixers came home for game three and were confident, maybe a bit too confident. The Lakers took charge from the first period and coasted to an easy, 111-101 victory, Abdul-Jabbar again dominating with 33 points and 14 rebounds, while the Doctor had 24 for the Sixers.

In game four it was the Sixers' turn. They came from behind and won it 105-102, behind Dawkins' 26 points and the Doctors' 23. Now it was back to Los Angeles for game five and it proved to be the Doctor's finest hour . . . but in a losing cause.

Once again the Lakers were outplaying Philly. With 9:01 minutes left in the game, the Lakers had an 89-77 lead. That's when Doc took over, just as he had in his ABA days, and the Sixers didn't seem to mind at all. He did everything, scoring 15 of the final 20 points for Philly, many of them on brilliant moves, a couple bordering on the impossible. In the end he had 36 points, but Abdul-Jabbar had 40 and the Lakers hung on to win, 108-103, giving them a 3-2 lead in the series.

However Los Angeles came out of it minus a center. Abdul-Jabbar had sprained an ankle late in the game, managed to finish, but now would miss game six. It seemed that Philly should be able to take the sixth at the Spectrum and force a showdown game in Los Angeles.

Yet somehow it didn't happen. The Lakers

showed a revamped lineup with Magic Johnson at center, and the rookie responded with an incredible game, scoring 42 points, getting 15 rebounds and seven assists, as the Lakers won the championship, 123-107.

It was a bitter disappointment for Julius and his teammates, and also for the fans, some of whom said the Sixers choked. But a team that loses its star, like the Lakers, often rally for one big effort without him, and Los Angeles did.

"Once we got to the finals our expectations were great," Julius said, "from the fans and mostly from ourselves. It's very disappointing to lose. We really expected to win this game and go to a seventh."

The Doctor had scored 27 points in the final game, doing all he could to try to win it. He still didn't have an NBA championship, but he had new-found respect, more fans than ever, and a new reinforcement that he was still the best forward in the league, and certainly the most exciting. After the season ended he won the Seagram's Award as the "most consistent and productive" player in pro basketball.

One sportswriter called him a champion without a ring, saying, "Julius Erving deserved the championship. Not the Sixers, obviously, just the Doctor." The writer went on to point out that Julius averaged 25.5 points against the Lakers, often while double and triple teamed. "Whenever any game was on the line, Erving had the ball. His presence made better players of Maurice Cheeks, Lionel Hollins, and Darryl Dawkins, the benefactors of the Lakers' defense, which was designed to stop Erving, at all costs."

Yet another writer pointed out that the Sixers

still didn't go to the Doctor enough, that he only got complete freedom when the team was behind late in the game, often too late to alter the outcome. He said that the Philly team would be better off if the offense always revolved around the Doctor.

"Being undemanding, even passive at times happens to be Erving's biggest, if only, flaw," the writer said, adding that if the Doctor were more selfish and assertive, the 76ers would be champs. He went on to say that no other superstar of the Doctor's magnitude would have been able to have such restraint in similar kinds of circumstances.

There could be something to that. The Doctor is one of the few superstars of the game who has never groused, sulked, or caused problems on his team. Because of that, he is one of the most popular and sought after athletes in the game, and he seems to relish his image as a nice guy, which he is. So he'll be back in Philly and the Sixers certainly have the youth and the talent to come back for another try.

And they still have Julius Erving. No matter what the outcome of subsequent title runs, no one can deny the Doctor his place in history. He is a future Hall of Famer and a man whose brilliance will never fade. No one can predict if there will be a better or more exciting forward some day. But one thing is for sure, there is only one Julius Erving, the Doctor, and there will never be anyone else like him in the game.

LARRY BIRD

In the midst of his rookie year with the Boston Celtics, when Larry Bird was constantly being touted as one of the best first-year players ever in the NBA, someone asked him if he had any plans when his playing days were over. That might seem to be a strange question to ask a guy whose pro career was just beginning, but Larry Bird had a ready answer.

"I'd like to coach junior high basketball back in French Lick," he said, quickly. "I've always said the best coaches should not be working in the pros, but in the grade schools. That's where the real coaching is needed."

French Lick is not the flavor of a new ice cream. It's the small town in Indiana where Larry Bird was born and grew up, and the place where his roots run deep. Naturally, he was asked why he wanted to return there.

"Because it's my home," he said. "It's the place where I feel most comfortable and where I want to raise a family someday. The people in French Lick want nothing from me and I want nothing from them. They treat me as just another guy, and that's how I want to be treated, more than anything."

If this sounds like an ending right at the beginning, it isn't. Rather, it shows the essence of the man, Larry Bird, who by the very nature of his current status, and the reverence given sports superstars, could go just about anywhere and remain a celebrity. But the 6-9 forward who can pass, rebound, and score with the best of them, isn't interested in pursuing the high life. His cousin, Ricky Johnson, explained why.

"Larry is the same exact guy I worked with in French Lick years ago," he said. "None of what has happened to him so far has changed him in the least, and I doubt if anything ever will. If I had his money and his name, I might be going out and having a pretty wild time. But all Larry wants to do is be the best basketball player around and help make the Celtics champions again."

Larry himself downplays the usual adjustments that NBA rookies must make to the pro game. His problems were in different areas.

"The only adjustment I've had to make is off the court," he says. "I'm not used to the traveling, the people crowding around me in restaurants and airports, and hassling with reporters."

In this day and age it's really unusual when a top athlete doesn't try to grab all the gusto at once. After all, the opportunities available to him are limitless, and since his peak earning years are relatively brief, why shouldn't he begin to set himself up for a career after he retires. That's why so many celebrities look for every possible opportunity to appear in the media, or in the right places with the right people.

In some ways, Larry Bird is a throwback to the old days, when ballplayers used to come out of small towns in the midwest or elsewhere, have brilliant careers, then disappear to those same towns. That, of course, was before the days of long-term, multi-year contracts, tax shelters, real estate investments, deferred payments, agents, lawyers, accountants, etc. that have since become associated with present-day superstars. Today, most of the star athletes who leave their small towns don't return.

In a sense, though, Larry Bird has always marched to the tune of a different drummer. He originally left French Lick for Indiana University, one of the country's best known major basketball schools. But he found the large campus just too overwhelming and withdrew before the basketball season started. That was the beginning of a year-long struggle to find himself, and when he emerged again, it was at Indiana State University.

Though not far in miles, Indiana State was considered a world away from Indiana University as far as basketball was concerned. That's what Larry wanted, and before he was through, he had the Sycamores ranked number one in the country and playing for the national championship. So in the words of a famous song, he did it his way.

Despite his collegiate success, there were detractors, individuals who said he wouldn't cut it in the pros, that he was too slow, he didn't jump well enough, and didn't have the quickness to play NBA defense. But, none of this bothered Larry, he just kept working at improving his game, a game based on team play and unselfishness. With that kind of determination, one wonders why some people thought he wouldn't make it in the pros.

But it is obvious that Larry Bird has the individual skills. Along with them, he also has a concept of how the game should be played, and that concept has its roots in the history of the game. Larry believes in loyalty and team play. His loyalty was tested when he was drafted as a junior eligible by the Boston Celtics. Yet he felt an obligation to his coach and teammates at Indiana State, and stayed for his senior year.

Then he joined the Celtics as the highest paid player in that proud franchise's history. The Celts had been the greatest winners in NBA annals. When Larry got there, the club was coming off two years of anarchy. And the rookie who was considered too slow helped transform them back into a team, and a leader in their division.

"I didn't want to go with a club that would be looking for me to put the ball up 25 times a night and be the big scorer," Larry said, a statement not many players in today's game could honestly make. To them, putting the ball in the hole is the name of the game. But to Larry, it was something different.

He would rather make the great pass than the great shot, and is capable of delivering the ball to a teammate in more ways than the post office can deliver mail. He can go behind his back, over his head, between his legs, and any other way that strikes him at the time. He can do it in full flight, off the dribble, or on the fast break. When you play with Larry Bird, you've got to be alert every second of the way.

"Larry's the best passing forward to come into the NBA in years, maybe ever," said "Hot Rod" Hundley, a former player and currently a broadcaster for CBS-TV. "Most people consider Rick Barry the best passing forward of modern times, but I think this kid is better. Larry looks for the pass first, whereas Barry usually looks for the shot. Bird has a great knack of drawing men to him and passing off at exactly the right second."

It is hard to argue about Larry's passing ability, especially with so many knowledgeable people commenting on it. For instance, former Celtic great Bob Cousy, considered one of the first really dynamic passers in the modern NBA, and the first to bring the art of passing to a large audience, put it very simply:

"Larry Bird is the best passer I've ever seen," said the Cooz. "In fact, he's so good he makes his teammates look good."

Remember, these comments are being made about a rookie, a first-year player who hasn't had many years of experience in honing his passing skills. He just came into the league and went to work. Not many players can go from College Player of the Year to NBA Rookie of the Year in one short season. But Larry Bird did it.

How did this shy and introspective man from a tiny town in Indiana become one of the kingpins of basketball? It may sound like a soap opera, but it isn't. The Larry Bird story is based on pure fact.

Larry was born in French Lick on December 7, 1956. He was one of six children and when he was very young, his parents divorced. His mother, Georgia Bird, had to work very hard just to put food on the table for her family. She often worked as a short-order cook, sometimes for as much as sixteen hours a day, leaving Larry pretty much to be raised by his grandmother. Life back then wasn't always easy.

French Lick is a community of about 2,000 people, which is considered a very small town no matter where it's located. There wasn't much for youngsters to do, so sports was always a big item. Larry began playing baseball and basketball early, with his older brothers acting as his first coaches.

It might surprise many to learn that basketball was such a popular sport in a small Indiana town, but the Hoosier state has been a hotbed for the court game for a long time. It is popular at the high school, college, and pro levels. In fact, there were pro teams in Indiana long before the present-day National Basketball Association came into existence.

During and immediately after World War II the National Basketball League and the Basketball Association of America struggled to make a go of it. When the leagues merged to form the NBA in 1949, there were pro franchises in Indianapolis and Fort Wayne. The Indianapolis team later disbanded and Fort Wayne moved its franchise to Detroit, but the present-day Indiana Pacers now operate out of Indianapolis. So the pros have always had a strong foothold in the Hoosier state.

At the college level the sport is also big time, with Indiana University, Purdue, and Notre Dame all competing within close proximity to one another. The smaller colleges also have active and enthusiastic programs, and have little difficulty filling their rosters with good players from the area high schools and junior colleges.

So, even in small towns such as French Lick, there was quite a hoop heritage. This meant that youngsters like Larry, learning the game for the first time, had ample opportunity along the way to learn it right. There was more emphasis placed on the pure form of the sport, on teamwork and passing, as opposed to the flashy one-on-one style that dominates the playgrounds of the large cities on the east and west coasts.

Tall and very thin as a youngster, Larry followed his older brothers, Mark and Mike, to the courts on many an afternoon, watching them play and soon joining them. He had to learn to play an intelligent game to compensate for going up against the bigger, stronger, and older boys. Finally reaching high school age, he attended Springs Valley High School where he eventually began to excel.

At Springs Valley, he met two fine coaches, Jim Jones and Gary Holland, both of whom were keenly interested in the youngsters and in the teaching of all the fundamentals and technical aspects of the sport. But they didn't always make it easy for them.

"They banged the fundamentals into us," Larry recalls. "If you made a mistake you did it over until you got it right. They were constantly drilling us on executing back doors, pick and rolls, and using the backboard for a layup. No fancy dan stuff or showboating."

Jones and Holland had instilled a sense of pride in Larry and they didn't have to prod him to practice and work on his game. He was doing that on his own.

"I never wanted to leave the court until I got everything just right. I would practice different kinds of moves for hours on end, and worked very hard to make my left hand as strong as my right. By then, my dream was to become a pro."

By his junior year Larry was filling out, getting stronger, and beginning to make his presence felt. He averaged sixteen points a game that year and was viewed as a player with a great deal of potential. In his senior year, the 1973-74 season, he was a shade over 6'-6" and looked outstanding right from the outset.

For the first time in his career he began exhibiting the all-around court play that would always characterize his game. He was not only scoring, but rebounding very well and passing like a guard. His play was totally unselfish and sometimes his coaches had to tell him to shoot more. But he always wanted every teammate involved in the action and he made sure they'd get the ball when they were open.

When the season ended, Larry had become a bona fide star, averaging 30.6 points a game, and adding the amazing total of 20.6 rebounds per contest, a very high number of boards for the relatively short, 32-minute high school game. He was still improving and it was obvious that he had a chance to be a fine college player.

There was little doubt that Larry had paid his dues. Even during his high school years he often spent long periods of time practicing by himself. Sometimes he'd work on his passing, not an easy thing to do when you're alone. But Larry would actually pass to himself, either using a wall, a fence, or anything else nearby. So it wasn't surprising when a number of colleges began recruiting him.

He wasn't deluged with recruiters as compared

to players from large high schools in the big cities were, but nevertheless there were some good ones after him. One school that bypassed him was the University of Kentucky, a perennial national power. It was said that the Kentucky coach, Joe B. Hall, felt Larry was too slow to play big-time college ball.

A Florida school reportedly wanted him, but Larry having never been on an airplane, refused to try one then. The school stopped pursuing him. That left three state schools with the best chance of getting him—Indiana, Indiana State, and Purdue.

Those three were more aware of his abilities than the out-of-state institutions. They weren't worried about his speed, lack of jumping ability, or anything else. Their scouts had seen him in action and knew he had to be good to earn the *Sunday Courier and Press* All-Area Player of the Year prize, which he got as a senior.

Indiana and Purdue were major powers, while Indiana State was a much smaller school that had been playing Division I ball for only a few years. Larry recalls liking the Indiana State campus and facilities, but he had already made his decision.

"I wanted to go to Indiana," he said. "That was always my first choice."

The Indiana coach was Bobby Knight, one of the best, but also one of the toughest in the business. He can often be very intimidating to young players and some wondered just how Larry would react to his sometimes harsh manner. But Larry didn't seem worried when he left for his first semester in the fall of 1974.

Suddenly, Larry found himself on a campus with

some 33,000 students. Coming from a town with barely over 2,000 inhabitants, he was somewhat awestruck. In fact, he found it very difficult to relax and settle into a normal lifestyle. The basketball season hadn't started, so he could not seek the one setting that would make him comfortable.

Things didn't get better, in fact, they got worse. After about a month, before basketball practice started, Larry suddenly left school, forfeiting his basketball scholarship and leaving his blossoming career up in the air. Confused, he returned to French Lick.

"I didn't like school," he said flatly. "And Indiana was just too big and I couldn't get adjusted. Sometimes now I wish I had stayed, but sometimes I don't."

Back home Larry enrolled in another school, Northwood Institute, a small junior college of 160 students in nearby West Baden, Indiana. The size of the school and the town seemed more to his liking, but after two months he was home again, having dropped out a second time.

"It just wasn't what I expected college to be," he recalls. "Plus I was just seventeen years old and hadn't been out on my own before. I guess all that just got to me."

Back in French Lick once more, Larry went out and got a job working for the town sanitation department. He drove a garbage truck, and after what had happened to him the previous three months, he was quite satisfied.

"It was the best job I ever had," he said. "I was with people all the time and very happy down there. My mom kept after me to think about returning to college. She wanted me to play ball and get an education, but at that point I didn't care what anyone said."

He might have decided against college at that time, but he hadn't given up on basketball entirely. He began playing for a nearby Amateur Athletic Union team. While he didn't have the same kind of feeling he would later get out of the sport, he played very well just the same. His team, based in the town of Mitchell, finally went to the state AAU tourney where Larry led them to victory and was named MVP. From there it was on to the nationals, where his club beat a team from Iowa as he scored 38 points and grabbed 35 rebounds, and was Most Valuable Player once again. His game certainly hadn't deteriorated, but he later said:

"I just couldn't really get the adrenalin flowing for the AAU games. It was the same kind of feeling I have in practice, not like a real game situation where you're playing for something."

During the year, his mother kept after him to think about returning to school. "The people in town never let Larry forget he had quit," she said, "and I didn't like that. I kept praying that something would happen and he'd go back to school somewhere."

A very traumatic experience during the year might have altered Larry's outlook on life. His father committed suicide, something that is not easy to accept no matter how close or far apart two people might be. But it's something that happened and to this day, Larry has never talked about it to reporters or media people.

Nearing the start of another school year Larry's attitude still had not changed. He seemed content working for the sanitation department and school wasn't given a second thought. But some people were thinking about him. The members of the coaching staff at Indiana State University, located some 90 miles away in Terre Haute, were interested.

Indiana State, a much smaller school than Indiana University, had roughly one-third the student body and a basketball team that was not constantly in the pressure cooker as was the case at Indiana. Still, the Sycamore cagers had a rather long and winning tradition.

The Sycamore's head coach was veteran Bob King, who had improved the basketball program at New Mexico, producing ten straight winning seasons and four post-season tournament appearances. A painful knee ailment caused him to retire in 1972, and two years later he was appointed Athletic Director of Indiana State.

"I was told that my prime concerns were getting the school into a conference, moving the football team into Division I and developing a winning basketball team."

The school had just opened a brand new arena, Hulman Center, which seated some 10,220 fans, and they wanted to fill it. But when the team completed its second consecutive 12-14 season in 1974-75, school officials decided to make another move. They replaced their present coach with Bob King. So the veteran was once again on the bench. After discussing the recruiting situation with his new assistants, Bill Hodges and Stan Evans, it was decided the first player they would pursue was Larry Bird.

So in late summer of 1975, Hodges and Evans

made the ninety mile drive to French Lick. They found Larry's house, rang the doorbell . . . but never got inside! Georgia Bird wouldn't let them in.

"She was standing behind the screen door and we told her who we were and what we had come for. Well, she looked at us and said something like, 'Why are you bothering him? He doesn't want to go to school. Just leave him alone.' "

Fortunately, the Indiana State coaches weren't about to give up so easily. They didn't want to return to Terre Haute without talking to Larry. If he was set against going to school, they wanted to hear it from him in person.

So they began searching for Larry. They figured French Lick wasn't that big and they'd be able to spot the blond-haired, 6'-9" youngster. There just couldn't be more than one of them out there. It didn't take them too long to find him. He was spotted coming out of a laundromat with his grandmother.

"We identified ourselves and at first he didn't seem to want to talk," recalls Hodges. "But we said we weren't there to pressure him, just to talk and tell him a few things about the school and the basketball program since Coach King had taken over. He finally consented to let us come over to his grandmother's house and we talked for an hour or so. He didn't agree to come there, but I felt sure that he would. About a week later he said he'd give it a try."

Once again Larry was going to give it a try. The happiest person was Georgia Bird, who later admitted she had turned the coaches away because of strict orders from her son.

"Larry had instructed me to tell anyone who

came that he wasn't available, so I told Coach Hodges just that. But I'm glad he didn't give up. His coming was like the answer to a prayer, because I knew that Larry had an awful lot of talent and he wasn't using it. He was just hanging around town, picking up garbage and painting park benches, and that wasn't the way I wanted him to spend the rest of his life."

It wouldn't be easy for Larry that first year at Indiana State, mainly because he wasn't eligible to play. He was officially a transfer, so he had to redshirt a year, an NCAA rule to prevent players from being induced to hop from one school to another. The fact that players have to sit out a season usually puts a stop to it.

In Larry's case he could practice with the team but couldn't participate, and for him this was very frustrating. Despite problems of the past year, he still felt confident in his basketball ability, and when he agreed to attend Indiana State, he told Bill Hodges:

"Indiana State may not be very good right now, but it will be when I get there."

Watching the team compile a mediocre 13-12 record in 1975-76 wasn't easy. But he got through the year and remained in school. When he returned for the 1976-77 season, he was in shape and raring to go.

"I've matured a lot and I'm ready to play," he declared. "I know what I want out of basketball now. As a 17-year-old I didn't know. Then last year, sitting out, I don't feel I improved half as much as I wanted, but I sat out two years waiting for this opportunity and I'm not going to blow it."

Coach King and his assistants felt the Sycamores had a strong team in 1976-77, though they weren't sure how strong. Larry, of course, had won a starting berth almost from the first day of practice. He was joined at forward by junior Harry Morgan, a 6'-7" leaper and good scorer. The center was 6'-11" junior, DeCarsta Webster, a Philadelphian who had come to Terre Haute via Miami Dade Junior College. The starting guards were 6' senior Danny King, and 6'-2" junior Jim Smith.

The team opened the season against Chicago State, not one of the college level basketball powers, but that didn't matter to the enthusiastic fans at Hulman Center. They had come to see the Sycamores and their new star forward. They weren't disappointed. On the basketball court Larry's shyness stopped. He had known from the first practice sessions that this was his team, that he had to lead, and his teammates also saw that he had the potential to take them a long way.

He wasn't bashful about putting the ball up, directing the offense, handling the ball when necessary, and encouraging his teammates to work. He often did this by example, as he pushed himself at the defensive end as hard as he did on offense.

When the game ended, Indiana State had an 81-60 victory, and they made it look easy. As expected, Larry was a standout, producing the kind of overall game only the great ones have. He led the team with 31 points, hitting on 13 of 29 shots from the floor and five of nine from the line. In addition, he had 18 rebounds, 10 assists, and three steals.

By the team's second game, the opposition already knew about him. St. Ambrose employed a box-and-one defense designed to stop Larry, and indeed, he just got 22 points on 10 for 19 shooting and a pair of free throws. But Indiana State breezed through with the score of 85-58, so Larry didn't have to do much more than that. He also collected another 16 rebounds, had 10 more assists, and four additional steals. After two games, he was already a star.

"Larry's really fluid," said Coach King, "and he's quicker than he appears. He can handle the ball and pass it like any guard in the country. In fact, he can pass it better than most of the guards in the country. And as far as I'm concerned, his strength is not in his scoring, but in his passing and rebounding."

As for Larry, he was generally pleased with his college debut. He was shooting just 48 percent from the field and wanted that to be better, saying he wouldn't be pleased unless he was over 60 percent, a near impossible figure for the type of shooter he was, but pointing out his constant desire to improve and achieve near perfection. He also talked about his defense, an aspect of the game which now meant a great deal to him.

"You've got to be able to play both ends of the court," he said. "If you hold your man to no points and you score two, you're going to win. I used to be pretty weak on defense because I never had it in my head how necessary it was and consequently I didn't want to play it badly enough. But when you're playing good defense you feel you're making a contribution, even if you make other mistakes, and that makes you feel better.

"Coach King has gotten us all brainwashed about defense. When I came here I was looking to play offense, mainly, but now I want to play defense. I take pride in it. We all do.

"Since I'm slower than a lot of guys, I've got to take some shortcuts to make up for it defensively. I'll try to keep my man from getting the ball as much as possible, and if he passes the ball, I try to make sure he doesn't get it back. Underneath I feel I can keep my man out and rebound with anyone. There's so much action going on underneath and I certainly like to be where the action is."

One of the things Larry really took pride in, even then, was his rebounding. Not a great leaper, he had to learn early how to get and maintain position, and how to judge where the ball was coming off. His 34 rebounds after two games were two more than center Webster, who was sixth in the nation a year earlier. Larry spoke about the friendly competition between the two.

"DeCarsta and I always go at it," he said. "I feel I've got to outrebound him. That's the first thing he checks on the stat sheet after the game. But I figure if I can beat him in rebounding this season, then next season he's going to work that much harder to beat me and we'll have a better team as a result."

Larry also talked about his willingness to adjust his game to different situations, with winning the ultimate goal.

"If I get the shot I'll take it," he admitted. "But if I don't, if the defense is worried about me too much, like in the St. Ambrose game, then I'll hit somebody else. If they start doing stuff like that box-and-one, I've got to pass off for us to win.

"I know I'm going to turn the ball over. I have to figure on about four turnovers a game, trying to squeeze passes inside and things like that. But I guess four isn't too bad considering how much I have my hands on the ball. I often find myself bringing the ball up the floor, and I will admit I feel better doing that because I like to be around the basketball."

The team won two more, then was derailed by a major opponent, Purdue, which beat the Sycamores, 82-68, as Larry popped in 27 points. Following that game, the club began rolling. Though they weren't playing nationally ranked teams, they were nevertheless winning and winning big. It became obvious that this was the best Sycamore team in the school's history.

When Indiana State whipped archrival West Texas State, the win streak stood at eight games. But West Texas slowed the ball down, trying to stop the Sycamore attack and the strategy almost worked. Indiana State pulled it out, 43-41, and Larry was held to his lowest game of the year, just 12 points on six of 21 shooting from the floor. It didn't matter, because the club won, but he was also about to embark on a scoring spree that would bring him his first taste of national headlines. Larry Bird was about to be introduced to the basketball world.

It started against Butler. Indiana State won easily, 90-67, as Larry had 42 points, shooting 16 of 29 from the floor and 10 of 11 from the line. Next he got 33 against Missouri Western, 47, a career high, against Missouri, St. Louis; 37 against Centenary, 40 twice in a row against Illinois State (the teams split back-to-back games), 37 against Wisconsin Parkside, 38 versus Cleveland State, 40 more against Eastern Michigan, and 45 big ones versus

Loyola of Chicago. During that period, the Sycamores lost only the one game to Illinois State.

During the streak, Larry averaged 39.9 points a game, and helped the Sycamores build their season record to 21-2. His overall average was up to 31.3, third best in the nation, and his rebounding average was 13.1, ninth best in the entire country. The only other player in the top ten in both categories was Bernard King of Tennessee.

In addition, his shooting percentage was up to 54 percent and his free throw mark at 83 percent. He was having a brilliant season and no one could deny him that, no matter who the Sycamores played.

The club took its final four games, as Larry tied his career high by getting 47 points against Butler, shooting 19 of 30 from the floor and nine of ten from the line. When the regular season ended, the club had a 25-2 mark, best in the school's history. But there was more excitement to come. Because of their great record, the Sycamores were invited to participate in the prestigious National Invitational Tournament, played at Madison Square Garden in New York.

To get there, the Sycamores had to win a first-round game against the University of Houston at the Hofheinz Pavilion in Houston. It wouldn't be easy. The Cougars were a major power, lead by a 6-4 all-American guard, Otis Birdsong, now an NBA star with the Kansas City Kings.

The game was nip and tuck all the way. Larry played brilliantly, living up to all his advance notice, once again he brought out the best in his teammates, as well. The game went right down to the wire with Houston winning it by a scant, 83-82 margin. But the Sycamores proved that they could play against the best.

Larry finished his season in fine style. He scored 44 points on 19 of 28 from the field and six of seven from the line, adding 14 rebounds along the way. He showed people once again that he was for real. In fact, Houston Coach Guy Lewis had this to say:

"Bird is the greatest player I've seen this year," adding, diplomatically, "other than ours." But everyone knew what he meant.

In 28 games, Larry had scored 918 points for a 32.8 average, and grabbed 373 rebounds for a 13.3 mark. He was third in the nation in scoring and seventh in rebounding, and just the 12th player in NCAA history to average over thirty points a game as a sophomore. In addition, he was a 54 percent shooter from the floor and an 84 percent man from the foul line.

After the season ended, he learned he had been named to the third team all-American by UPI and was honorable mention in the AP poll. He was a second team choice of the United States Basketball Coaches Association, and finished tenth in the AP balloting for College Basketball Player of the Year. It had truly been a great season for him.

During the summer, Larry participated with a United States team that won the gold medal at the World University Games in Europe. He obviously had conquered his fear of flying, but that didn't mean he enjoyed traveling. He remained a small-town boy at heart, and when asked what he liked most about his trip to Europe, Larry replied:

"Landing at the Terre Haute airport when I came home."

Then it was back to Indiana State for the 1977-

78 season. The Sycamores had basically the same cast of characters returning and were hoping for another big season. They began in fine fashion, whipping Westmont, 88-54, with Larry getting 29. The next game was a big one. They would meet Purdue once more, a team they had to beat if they hoped to achieve any kind of respectability.

The Sycamores played their best game of the year, blowing the Boilermakers out of the arena, 91-63. And they did it without a great performance from Larry, who made just 11 of 31 shots and finished with 26 points. He did contribute in other ways, with 17 rebounds and eight assists, but the Sycamores had won a big game as a team, and everyone was happy.

The team was unbelievable, beating every team they met, many times by substantial margins. Some of their winning scores were 84-68, 102-55, 102-76, 82-50, and 78-59. With the record of 13-0, the little school from Terre Haute was making a name for itself. Ranked as high as sixth nationally in one of the major polls, they were featured in an article in *Sports Illustrated* magazine.

Larry, of course, was at the center of the article as well as the center of the team. He was playing very well again, though his scoring and rebounding stats were down just a shade from the year before, indicative of more contributions from his teammates. As the magazine story said:

"He continues to be just about the best-passing, quickest-thinking and smoothest-operating big man in the country. Bird plays with instinct and intelligence, moving adroitly without the ball, following his shots and making important steals. He is a complete player."

But just as it seemed the Sycamores were writing the basketball Cinderella story of the year, the bubble burst. The team lost a 79-76 decision to Southern Illinois, despite 38 points by Larry. Two nights later they were beaten by Illinois State, 81-76, a game in which Larry canned 37. An overtime loss to Wichita State, an eight-point loss to Creighton, and a three-point defeat by Loyola of Chicago followed. Inexplicably, the Sycamores had dropped five in a row.

It was hard to determine what quite happened. There were no injuries, just a team slump, and while many of the losses were close, the club certainly wasn't playing the kind of dominant ball that they had during their long win streak. Larry averaged over thirty points during the losses, and seemed to be his old self. Perhaps the club had just played over its head.

Larry had already reached the point where he didn't talk to the press much. Not a big talker by nature, he claimed he had been misquoted at times and now preferred keeping a low profile. But, when he did talk it was about basketball and basketball only! Personal questions were strictly off limits.

"Basketball is my whole life," he told one writer. "I don't want to talk about the past or the future." Especially, for example, personal questions like "Who's your girl friend?" or "What does your brother do?" or "What are you doing tomorrow?" Ask him those type of questions and you got no response.

Rival coaches, however, never hesitated to talk about Larry. Tom Apke of Creighton, was one of his real admirers.

"Larry is a totally creative player," said Apke.

"Being a great passer, he can create many kinds of things that other big scorers can't. I first saw him during the tryouts for the World University Games team. Many of the great college players in the country were there and they played a series of games among themselves. Larry's team won most of them mainly because of his unselfish play."

The losing streak ended with a victory over West Texas State, but the club didn't have its early season dominance. Splitting their next four games, they then won three in a row to close out the regular season. Now participating in the Missouri Valley Conference, they were headed to the conference tournament to determine which club qualified for a berth in the NCAA playoffs. A win would mean the losses at midseason wouldn't matter.

The first game was against West Texas State and the Sycamores won, 90-71, with Larry getting 27. He canned 33 more in an 88-81 victory over Bradley, then popped for 40 as the Sycamores whipped New Mexico State, 80-78, in double overtime. They now faced Creighton for the MVC crown.

The Creighton Club had already defeated the Sycamores twice during the regular season. They slowed the action down, keeping Larry from going on one of his patented scoring sprees and leading the fast break. The game stayed close, and in the end Creighton pulled off a 54-52 victory.

Disappointed with their 11-5, second-place finish in the conference, the Sycamores returned home, only to learn the team had received another NIT bid. So once again there was a chance to salvage some national recognition out of what had turned into a dismal season.

They won their opening game, defeating Illinois

State, 73–71, Larry getting 27 points and ten rebounds. But in their quarterfinal contest, they were beaten by a point, with Rutgers doing the trick, 57–56. They had come up short once again. Now the season *was* definitely over.

After the fine, 25–3, record of the previous year, the team finished the 1977–78 season with a 23–9 mark. It was still a good one, but far below expectations, especially after the 13-game win streak at the start of the season. After that, they were 10–9 the rest of the way, and that's a rather mediocre mark.

As for Larry, he had put together another sensational season, scoring 959 points in 32 games for a 30.0 average. He was a 53 percent shooter from the field and grabbed 369 rebounds for an 11.5 per game norm. Forward Harry Morgan had been an 18.6 scorer, after him the next player was at 6.3. A marked lack of balance on offense might have been the problem.

But none of that could mask Larry's greatness. He was the Missouri Valley Conference Most Valuable Player and an unanimous all-league selection. And this time the national boys didn't ignore him. He was a first-team consensus all-America, being named by the AP, UPI, and all the other major polls. In addition, he was second in the nation in scoring, was runner-up in the UPI Player of the Year balloting (by the college coaches), and third in the AP Player of the Year voting (by sportscasters and writers). It was safe to say he toiled in obscurity no longer.

With three of the team's starters graduating, it was hard to say what the next season would bring. Larry would have an entirely new supporting cast.

But then again, there was still some doubt whether Larry Bird would be back himself.

For one thing, he was now a junior eligible in the NBA draft. This was because his original class would be graduating, Larry losing a year when he dropped out of Indiana back in 1974. At any rate, being a junior eligible meant that an NBA team could draft him, but any attempt to sign him could not be done until the following year. Drafting him would be a gamble, since the club would have to wait a year (giving up a chance to grab a player who could sign immediately), and if they couldn't sign him by a certain date, then they'd lose him anyway. Of course, Larry could get around the junior eligible business by declaring "hardship" and making himself available immediately. But he showed no inclination to do that.

It was not considered a banner year for draftees, but still, any teams interested in eligible juniors usually waited for a later round. Portland had the first pick that year and took 6'-10" Mychal Thompson of Minnesota. Kansas City followed by picking Phil Ford, and they were followed by Indiana, which took Rick Robey. The New York Knicks took Michael Ray Richardson, followed by the Golden State Warriors, who chose Purvis Short of Jackson State.

The sixth pick belonged to the Boston Celtics, and their wily general manager, Red Auerbach, stepped up to the microphone and stunned everyone by saying:

"Boston takes Larry Bird of Indiana State!"

The choice took most people by surprise. Immediately, the reporters descended, trying to find out if there was some kind of deal, or if Larry intended to declare hardship. No, he told them, he had no intention to turn pro.

"I intend to get my degree," he said, "and I feel I owe Coach King and my teammates one more year."

Ironically, the very reason Auerbach chose Larry was for his unselfish attitude and team-oriented style. The Redhead was striving to rebuild his once-proud franchise and was willing to take the gamble. He didn't expect Larry to sign, but he wanted the first crack at him after the 1978-79 season.

So it was back to Indiana State for his senior year. Before the season started, Larry and his teammates were in for a big shock. Coach King had become ill and doctors told him he probably wouldn't be able to coach that season. Assistant Bill Hodges was appointed interim coach, and later in the season head coach, while King remained at ISU as Athletic Director. So the club not only had its new players, but a new coach as well.

Starting along with Larry would be 6'-3" junior guard, Carl Nicks, who seemed to excel in his position; 6'-7½" Alex Gilbert, a forward-center who had great leapability, 6'-8" forward Brad Miley, and 6'-2½" guard Steve Reed. Bob Heaton and Leroy Staley were reliable subs. The remainder of the bench was weak, and only Bird and Staley were seniors.

In effect, the team was also operating without a legitimate center. The past two seasons DeCarsta Webster had been in the middle, and despite some deficiencies, he was a 6'-11" presence. Neither Gilbert nor Miley were really pivotmen. Gilbert, by virtue of his leaping ability would undoubtedly have to guard the taller players, and everyone would have to box out and hit the boards.

So, in some ways it seemed that Larry would have to carry an even greater load as a senior. He was the best scorer, best rebounder, best passer, tallest starter, and often brought the ball upcourt. It looked as if he'd have to be a magician for the team to approach its performances of the past two seasons.

The team opened with an easy, 99–56, victory over Lawrence, and Carl Nicks showed that he was going to be a valuable asset, giving the club an outside scoring threat to go with Larry. He was the leading scorer with 27 points, and Gilbert topped the rebounders with 15. Purdue was next to meet the Sycamores and everyone figured Bird and company would get their comeuppance.

It never happened. Indiana State won the game with relative ease, 63–53, Larry once again showing his great all-around ability, leading the way with 22 points and 15 rebounds. The Sycamore odyssey had begun.

Soon, the team was beating everyone in sight. During the seven-game stretch starting five games into the season, the club averaged 100 points a game, with Larry accounting for 34.4 per game during that span. People were beginning to take notice, as the Sycamores were now in the top 20 and starting the slow climb toward the top.

More people were also taking notice of Larry Bird. Since being drafted by the Celtics, he became well known, and when a sports figure is well known, he often goes under the microscope of the press and media.

"Playing basketball is supposed to be fun,"

Larry said, "but if I had to spend an hour or so every day talking to reporters, I wouldn't have time for much else."

With Larry doing the silent Sam bit, reporters began approaching other members of the team and asked questions about their superstar leader. This, of course, could not continue, causing the locker room to be closed to the press and Coach Hodges handling the media.

On the court, it was a different story. There was no shyness, no holding back there. Larry was doing everything, and with more assurance than in past seasons. Though doubled and sometimes triple teamed, he continued to score and rebound. Offensively, he was a multi-dimensional player, with the ability to loft 20 to 25 foot jump shots with great accuracy. Yet he could go to the hoop and work in close with either hand, using a variety of shots and moves.

His passing continued to border on the spectacular throughout the games. He would often throw one way while looking the other, or needle the ball through a maze of players to a teammate for an easy hoop. As one coach said, "Bird seems to have a knack of seeing guys before he even gets the ball."

Though not a great leaper by any means, his positioning on rebounds was uncanny, as he continued to lead the Sycamores in that category by a wide margin. There was still some doubt that he wouldn't be able to get away with that in the NBA because the opposition would be bigger, stronger, and smarter. But Celtic GM Red Auerbach, who now had a vested interest in Larry and was watching him carefully, disagreed.

"Larry gets up high enough," said Auerbach. "Bill Russell was the greatest rebounder the game has ever known and he always told me that 80 percent of all rebounds were grabbed below the rim."

So the legions of Bird fans were growing. Larry wasn't getting *all* the headlines, however. Michigan State had a 6-8 sophomore guard named Earvin "Magic" Johnson who was also dazzling fans and coaches with his ballhandling and passing. No one knew it then, but the two were heading for a showdown meeting and comparisons that would continue right into the pros.

And the Sycamores kept winning. There was a close, overtime victory over New Mexico State, 91-89, with Larry getting 37, and a one-pointer against Southern Illinois. But many of their other victories were one-sided, and as the season moved into its latter stages, the Sycamores were moving up in the national rankings, with some speculation that they were one of the very best teams in the country.

In the final game of the regular schedule, Larry scored a career high 49 points against Wichita State, bringing him headlines once again. There were still skeptics, for example, this one report from a midwestern paper.

"Wichita State, Ball State, Morris Harvey, Cleveland State . . . what kind of a schedule is that! People are saying that Indiana State has the best team in the country and the best player in Larry Bird. But who have they beaten? What all-Americans has Bird gone up against? I'm not saying the team isn't that good, but it seems that both team and star must still do it against the big boys."

Plenty of people shared that opinion. The Sycamores had defied all logic and won 26 straight games. They had risen to the number one spot in the polls, but it was solely by virtue of the fact that all the other Division I schools had been beaten. And that's what it took to get them up there. Now they'd have to do it all over again at the upcoming Missouri Valley Conference tournament hopefully, followed by the NCAA playoffs.

The MVC tourney wasn't difficult. The Sycamores under Bill Hodges had blended into a fine unit, finding ways to compensate for their weaknesses with the other players accepting secondary roles to Larry and working everything off of him. It seemed as if someone would expose their limitations, but it just hadn't happened yet.

So the Sycamores whipped West Texas State, 94–84, then took Southern Illinois, 79–72. Then came the title game with New Mexico State. The Sycamores played solid ball once more, Larry scored 20, and they won the MVC title, 69–59. But the win was a costly one. Larry came out of a scramble underneath with a badly injured left thumb. X-Rays taken after the game revealed the worse, the thumb was fractured in three places. The Sycamores had finally qualified for the NCAA Tournament and now might lose their superstar forward, which would undoubtedly mean instant elimination.

What no one counted on was Larry's determination. He checked with team trainer Bob Behnke, who said he couldn't damage the thumb anymore by playing. Larry made his decision. He told the trainer to just wrap the thumb with a tight bandage instead of putting it in a cast. He would play.

"Larry Bird is the toughest athlete I've seen in eighteen years in the game," Bob Behnke said. "Most guys would have been sitting and watching after an injury like that. But not Larry. He didn't give sitting a second thought."

So the Sycamores would face Virginia Tech in their first playoff game. They won it easily, 86–69, as Larry and Carl Nicks shared high scoring honors with 22 points each, and Larry grabbing 14 rebounds. The thumb seemed to be holding up. He was playing in a great deal of pain, not being able to grip the ball as well with his left hand, but he was still doing the job and the Sycamores were playing with confidence and assurance. More people were becoming believers with each passing day.

After Virginia Tech, the Sycamores went up against a good Oklahoma team and they blew them out. The Sooners stayed close for thirteen minutes or so, but their center, Al Beal, had to sit out with three fouls, and ISU took full advantage of the situation. Larry began scoring, and along with Alex Gilbert, controlled the boards, enabling the Sycamores to increase a 33–30 lead to 45–37 at the half.

In the second half, Indiana State began pouring it on. Larry continued to play well in spite of his thumb, and got plenty of help from his teammates, especially Carl Nicks, who had matured into a fine player, perhaps the only other one on the club besides Larry with pro potential. By the buzzer, it was a 93–72 game, as Larry scored 29 points, had five assists, and 15 rebounds.

Now the club was in the Midwest Regional final, just three games away from the national championship and an undefeated season. But standing in their way was Arkansas, led by their 6-5 all-American guard, Sidney Moncrief. The Razorbacks were definitely one of the better teams in the country. To many, this would represent the first real test the Sycamores had all year.

Arkansas knew they would have to do something about Larry Bird if they were to have a good chance, and their coach, Eddie Sutton, talked about it before the game.

"You're not going to stop him," Sutton said, "but you can slow him down. He hurts you most with his passing. In fact, he's the best passer for a big man I've ever seen. What we've got to do is try to take the pass away from him."

With the Razorbacks concentrating on keeping Larry from hitting open men, the big guy simply shifted his own tactics and started hoisting up the shots himself. Some seven minutes into the second half, Larry had 25 points and the Sycamores had a lead. Finally, Arkansas changed tactics. Sutton decided to put his star player, Moncrief, on Larry.

Moncrief wasn't as big, but he was quicker than Larry and he began fronting him, denying him the ball. The Sycamores had difficulty adjusting and Arkansas began pecking away at the lead, tying the game at 71-all with less than two minutes remaining. Suddenly it was anybody's game.

The Razorbacks had the ball and decided to hold for the last shot. But with 1:08 left, they turned it back over to Indiana State. Now they held, hoping to get Larry to take the final shot. With eleven seconds on the clock, Larry got the ball, but Moncrief remained all over him. He managed to pass to guard Steve Reed, who then got the ball to forward Bob Heaton. Heaton put up a left-handed layup which bounced around the rim and dropped through.

With two seconds left, Arkansas was helpless. Indiana State had won again, 73–71, and now it was to Salt Lake City and the Final Four. Despite playing again in constant pain, Larry had led his team with 31 points and 10 rebounds, and he was getting additional plaudits.

"Fundamentally, Larry is as good as any player to come out of college in a long time," said another coach. "He reminds me of Dave DeBusschere the way he digs underneath, but in other ways he can do more than DeBusschere. I don't see how he can't help but be a great pro."

His own coach, Bill Hodges, called Larry "the smartest player I've ever seen. He seems to have a built-in radar which directs where and when to pass and shoot."

So the Sycamores moved on to Utah, where they joined Michigan State, DePaul, and the University of Pennsylvania as the four remaining teams seeking the national title. In their semi-final game, Larry and friends would come up against a very sound DePaul team, one that wanted to win it for their 65-year-old coach, Ray Meyer.

The game was very close in the first half, tied on fifteen separate occasions, with neither team able to get more than a four-point lead. While Larry was shooting very well and putting on his usual passing show, keen observers began to detect the thumb giving him increasing trouble, especially with his overall ball control.

It was still an extremely close game, but the Sycamores put on a spurt and extended a three-point lead to eleven after 3:32 had elapsed. For a few minutes, their fans envisioned them breaking it open. But then they began turning the ball over and let DePaul get back into the game. It was 67--61 when the Blue Demons hit six baskets in six trips down the floor, giving them a 73–71 lead with just 4:59 left. Could the Sycamores be crumbling under the pressure?

When Larry missed a shot, DePaul got the rebound and went into a four-corners stalling offense. That might have been a mistake, because they turned it over and Bob Heaton hit a layup off a pass from Larry to tie it. DePaul hit a free throw for a one-point lead with 1:37 left, but Nicks came back with a pass to Heaton for another hoop, making it 75–74.

DePaul went to its freshman star, Mark Aguirre, who missed a 20-footer. Leroy Staley grabbed the rebound for the Sycamores and was fouled. He hit a free throw to make it 76–74, and that's the way it ended. The Sycamores had taken their 33rd straight victory, and it put them into the NCAA finals.

Larry had another brilliant game, with 35 points on 16 of 19 from the floor, outstanding shooting. He also had 16 rebounds and nine assists. But astute Bird-watchers felt the thumb was paining him even more, and they pointed out that he hadn't scored in the final 7:32 of the game, and what's more, had committed eleven turnovers.

"Eleven turnovers!" Larry exclaimed. "If I had known I would do that I'd have thought we'd lose the game. We were lucky today, I guess, very lucky."

Now he'd have just two days to rest the thumb before the final game against the Spartans of Michigan State, the team that featured Magic Johnson and Greg Kelser. Since Johnson and Bird were considered the two best players in college ball, the game received a tremendous media build-up and a huge national television audience tuned in to watch it happen.

Michigan State made their plans to cage the Bird. Coach Jud Heathcote devised what he called a "matchup zone," which, in effect, put "a man and a half on Bird." In other words, one man was on him all the time, and another was usually dropping off to help. Along with this, the Spartans would try to cut off as many of the passing lanes as they could. It was easy for them to practice this, because Magic Johnson played much in the same way as Larry.

So the Spartans came into the game prepared and they had the pieces to tie up the puzzle. Magic Johnson and Greg Kelser were superstars, but the rest of the cast proved more competent than the Sycamore supporting cast. Michigan State took the lead five minutes into the game and never relinquished it.

Early in the second half, Spartan guard Terry Donnelly hit on four straight jump shots increasing the lead to 16. The Sycamores continued struggling, but couldn't really make a go of it. They cut it to 61-54 at one point, then got the ball four straight times and didn't score.

It was a frustrating game for Larry. He didn't look sharp. Perhaps it was the thumb, all the tough tournament play making it more painful, or perhaps it was just an off game. The Spartans certainly had something to do with it. On a number of occasions he was heard yelling to his teammates, "Give me the ball! Give me the ball!" But they couldn't get it to him.

The final score was 75-64. Michigan State was the national champs. Their star, Magic Johnson, scored 24 points and was named the tourney's MVP.

As for Larry, neither he nor his teammates had anything to be ashamed of. They finished a remarkable 33-1 season and had come a lot further than anyone in the country could have imagined. Larry scored just nineteen points in the final game, yet with his bad thumb and all, he grabbed fifteen rebounds.

"I feel more sorry for my teammates than I do for myself," he said, afterwards. "I would have liked very much to win, but now I can look forward to next year."

There was plenty to look back upon also. In 34 games in 1978-79, Larry averaged 28.6 points and 14.9 rebounds, making him the nation's number two scorer and fourth best rebounder. He also finished his career in fifth place on the all-time NCAA scoring list behind Pete Maravich, Freeman Williams, Oscar Robertson, and Elvin Hayes, some pretty fast company.

Needless to say, he was all everything, from a consensus all-America to the Player of the Year on all the polls. In three years he had led the Sycamores to an 81-13 overall mark, and an incredible 50-1 record at Hulman Center. He had surely succeeded in helping to fill the building, as school officials hoped.

He also left Indiana State with something else—a diploma. Sticking to his word, Larry had continued working hard all four years and despite never really caring much for schoolwork, graduated with a Bachelor of Science degree in Physical Education.

There was also the future to think about. Larry was well aware that he could command a rather hefty contract, given the market and the circumstances of his outstanding college career. One thing bothered him, though, and it was something he did feel compelled to speak up about. Many people were beginning to refer to him as a "Great White Hope," with the intimation that a white superstar would be welcomed royally in a sport where the majority of top players were now black.

"I don't think of myself as any kind of Great White Hope," he said. "To me, that implies racism. From what I've seen all players, black and white, blend well in the NBA. People tend to forget that on the whole the blacks are the best basketball players in the world. I think it's because they're hungrier. They crave success. A lot of white kids are too spoiled. They get cars and other luxuries. But it seems as if this whole black-white thing is being overblown. Fans are all the same. They just want to see good basketball and have a winner, no matter what the color of the players."

Larry certainly wasn't spoiled, not the way he worked at his game. Aware that he was going into the big time, he knew he'd need an agent, and he worked at that too, with a little help from his friends. A committee of five knowledgeable people from Terre Haute agreed to help him with the selection of someone to represent him. After screening more than forty people, they selected Bob Woolf, an attorney from Boston, and one of the most respected men in his field. Woolf immediately got to work and opened negotiations with the Celtics.

When he was drafted by the Celts, Larry knew right away that he was ticketed for a franchise with an incredible history. The Celtics had dominated their sport in a way no other team ever had. Since the league was formed in 1946, Boston had won the championship some thirteen times, more than any other club.

It started in 1956 when the team acquired rookie center Bill Russell from the University of San Francisco, and Russell proceeded to become the finest defensive big man in the game's history. With Russell, Coach Red Auerbach was fully able to utilize the talents of his other stars, beginning with Bob Cousy and Bill Sharman, and going from there to Tom Heinsohn, Frank Ramsey, Sam Jones, K.C. Jones, Satch Sanders, John Havlicek and many others.

The Celts became the epitome of the basketball "team," with everyone working equally hard and playing whatever roles they had to in order to win. St. Louis won the title in 1957-58 when Russell hurt an ankle, but then the Celtics ripped off eight straight, an amazing mark. The Philadelphia 76ers broke through in 1967-68, but the Celts got two more after that, giving them ten world championships in eleven years, and eleven titles in thirteen seasons. They added two more in 1973-74 and 1975-76, as the team was rebuilt around another hustling center, Dave Cowens.

Through it all, the years of the Celtic dynasty, Celtic pride was legendary. "We hated to lose two games in a row," Cousy once said. "No matter what part of the season, we never coasted. We wanted to win them all."

The formula was always the same: a fastbreaking offense, tenacious defense, strong rebounding, a strong bench featuring a traditional sixth man who could come off the pines and lift the whole team. Frank Ramsey was the first to play that role, and John Havlicek the best known.

Auerbach eventually retired as coach, but continued to run the team as General Manager, and through careful drafting and some shrewd deals, he kept the team at a continued high level of quality. Then in 1977, the ownership changed and things began going downhill. Auerbach suddenly didn't have control anymore and at one point almost left the club. The team slid from a 44-38 season in 1976-77, to successive seasons of 32-50 and 29-53, total disasters.

There was just no stability, with coaching changes and many personnel moves. Then in 1979, Harry Mangurian became the sole owner and immediately turned the control of the club back to Auerbach. By the time he took to signing Larry Bird, he felt he had the club back on track.

But that wouldn't be easy. Suddenly, agent Woolf and GM Auerbach found themselves miles apart. The two had tangled before and were very adept at playing the game. It is said that Woolf was asking for a multi-year pact calling for about $1 million a year, while Auerbach countered with an offer at around $400,000. If those sound like huge numbers, they just reflect the current inflated market values on ballplayers.

At any rate, the negotiations began turning bitter, and at one point they actually broke off. Because Larry had been drafted as a junior eligible, the rule stated that the Celts had to sign him by June 25, or he'd go back into the regular draft and another team could pick him. The date was rapidly approaching.

Finally, Celtic owner Harry Mangurian stepped in and raised the ante sharply. That encouraged Woolf to come down a bit and finally an agreement was reached. Larry Bird's first professional contract called for about a $3.25 million spread over five years, which comes to about $650,000 a season, making Larry not only the highest paid Celtic rookie ever, but the highest paid Celtic ever.

Now it was time for basketball once again. The Celts also had a new coach in 1979-80. He was Bill Fitch, who can be both very funny and very tough. His philosophy jibed with Auerbach's and the Celtics went about returning to the successful formula of the past.

It didn't take long to see that it was working. Early in the preseason Larry showed he was the real thing. Those critics who felt he would be too slow for the pro game proved wrong. He was making his shots, rebounding very well, running the break, and still throwing his marvelous, exciting passes.

"I guess the key to my game is that I always know what's happening on the court, and that means I have to know what I can and can't do. For instance, I try to learn about each guy who's going to defend me, so I know how I can score on that particular guy. As for my passing, I just see a situation and respond to it. It's instinct more than anything else, I guess."

The team had obviously regained the balance of past seasons. Cowens and Archibald looked better than they had in two or three years. Cedric Maxwell was still improving, and like Larry, was an unselfish player. So was M.L. Carr, whose role it was to come off the bench. Chris Ford was steady, though not spectacular, and the rest of the bench seemed ready.

Larry, of course, earned a starting berth quickly, and it soon became obvious to the entire league that Bird had arrived and the Celtics were back. They broke atop the Atlantic Division of the Eastern Conference with their archrivals, the Philadelphia 76ers, in hot pursuit. The fans held their breaths. The team had been so bad just a year earlier that the fans couldn't believe the turnaround. Once again, they rocked ancient Boston Garden to the rafters.

By the time the team had won eleven of its first fourteen games the fans were back and the players knew they had recaptured the touch as well. Larry had fit in very well. After fourteen games he was averaging close to twenty points, ten rebounds, and five assists a game, leading the club in the first two categories. And his influence could be felt in the way the other players looked at things, such as when veteran Cowens said:

"We have players who aren't concerned with egos, who are willing to pass the ball, to work for one goal. That's the difference in our team this year."

Four games later, in a 118–103 Celtic victory over Indiana, Larry had one of his finest outings, scoring 30 points, grabbing 11 rebounds, and adding three assists and two steals. It was beginning to feel like college days all over again.

"The only way to play Larry is strong outside

and front him inside," said Indiana coach Bobby Leonard. "He has a great nose for the ball and we didn't play him strongly enough outside. Once he gets two steps with the ball, the chances are he'll score."

Larry did have seven turnovers in the game, but explained it the same way he explained his turnovers at Indiana State. "You can't be a perfectionist when you thread the needle on passes or shoot from outside," he said. "You just have to have confidence enough and most of your game will be effective."

He did suffer a small crisis in confidence a short time later when he went into a brief shooting slump. His reaction was to almost stop shooting altogether. But Fitch stepped in quickly and with a firm hand. He told the rookie flat out, "Players with confidence in their shot don't stop shooting." So Larry started popping again, but still vowed to improve his shot during the off-season. Though he might not have been satisfied with his play, others were more than satisfied.

"Larry is a lot like Bob Cousy in that he has extraordinary court sense," said assistant coach K.C. Jones, a former teammate of Cousy. "He creates opportunities, patiently allows them to develop, then capitalizes on them. Like Cooz, Larry sometimes gives the impression that he's hot-dogging it, but that's not true. He appears that way because he's so gifted, and only a gifted player can make those near-impossible passes. It's funny, when I compare Larry to Cooz I sometimes forget that Cooz was 6'-1" and a guard, while Larry is a 6'-9" forward. When you combine his passing with his speed, scoring, savvy, strength, and dedication, you have to say that Larry Bird has the potential to be the greatest all-around forward ever to play this game."

Of course, Larry's old rules prevailed regarding interviews. No personal questions, so the impressions of him were that he was shy and withdrawn, standoffish, and perhaps even a snob. His agent, Bob Woolf, who had also become a good friend, tried to dispel that notion.

"Larry's so different in private than he is in public that it's a shame more isn't known about that side of him," Woolf said. "I really love this kid. He's so down to earth and so intelligent that I wish more people could know what he's about. But he's shy around strangers, especially reporters.

On the court, Larry was anything but shy, and he was helping the Celtics write an incredible story. As the season neared the halfway mark, not only was the team still atop their division, but they had the best record in the entire league. If they kept up the pace they would complete the greatest single-season turnaround in league history.

There was a humorous side to the Celtic pace. When someone asked Larry about the most difficult adjustment he had to make coming into the NBA, his answer was a shocker.

"Losing," he said. "I can't get used to losing so much. I've never lost so much in one season as we have already."

At the time of the question, the Celts had lost about twelve games, fewer than any other team, yet because of the great seasons at Indiana State and, of course, the much longer pro season, Larry was on his losingiest team ever.

In late January, Larry bailed the Celts out with

some clutch shooting, increasing his career-high to 36 points as Boston whipped the San Diego Clippers. He learned soon afterwards, that he had been named to the Eastern all-star squad and would be participating in his first NBA All-Star Game.

Larry's old college rival, Magic Johnson, who was also having a brilliant rookie year, was a starter for the West squad, while Larry was a sub for the East. It was a typical all-star game, with a lot of shooting and questionable defense. They're usually high scoring affairs, which is what the fans enjoy.

During his first couple of stints in the game Larry didn't do much. Still the East had a 17-point lead in the final period . . . and they blew it! The West fought back to tie the score at 126–all with just 37 seconds left in regulation time. East coach Billy Cunningham then sent Larry back into the game.

Larry quickly got the ball and rifled a 22-foot pass inside to Moses Malone for a layup. But with 17 seconds left, Paul Westphal tied it for the West once again. With time running out, Larry took a 20-footer, and missed. The game went into overtime and it was at this time that Larry really took over.

With 2:29 left, he fed Malone again for a short jumper to give the East a 134–132 lead. With 2:00 left, he hit on a 20-footer of his own to make it 136–134, East. With 1:40 on the clock he took a long shot from three-point range, and made it! Now the score was 139–136, and with just seconds left he rebounded a missed shot and passed in one motion to George Gervin for a lay-up that iced the game at 144–136. As one writer covering said:

"Larry Bird didn't play the most minutes, he didn't score the most points, he didn't get the MVP. He just won the game."

The respect for the rookie was growing. Shortly after the All-Star Game he got 33 in a Celtic victory over Utah, and Jazz coach Tom Nissalke called him "a great player already, the best to come into the pros since Bill Walton."

He got a new career high, a 45-point effort against the Phoenix Suns. There didn't seem to be any limit to what he could do on the court. In mid-March he had 29 points in a one-sided victory over the Nets, which brought the Celts record to 56–18. With eight games remaining in the season, they still led the Sixers by two. Afterwards, the N.J. Nets coach Kevin Loughery talked of the Celtics amazing turnaround:

"The one most dazzling aspect of their game is Larry Bird," Loughery said. "He's the only starter different from last year, so basically, it's the same team as last year. But their overall attitude, their ability to pass, their confidence—as far as I'm concerned you can trace it all to Bird's presence."

Coach Fitch also picked that night to talk about his prize rookie. "He's a lot better now than he was three months ago," Fitch said. "He makes a move every once in a while that makes you want to say, 'Holy cow!' I think you have to consider him for the MVP along with Doctor J., and Abdul-Jabbar."

The season ending, Boston took its division with a 61–21 mark, the best in the league. Philly finished at 59–23, while the L.A. Lakers, the team Magic Johnson had gone to, finished at 60–22 in the Pacific Division of the Western Conference. They were the three best teams in the League.

As for Larry, he had put together a sensational rookie year. Playing in all 82 games, he scored 1,745 points for a 21.3 average, 16th best in the league and tops on the Celtics. He also led the team in rebounding with 852 boards, a 10.4 mark and 10th best in the league. He had 370 assists, second on the club to Archibald, but there was no way to measure all the dazzling passes and great plays that had broken games open or inspired the rest of the club to start rolling.

No one could predict whether or not Larry would win the Rookie of the Year prize. Magic Johnson, as mentioned, also had an outstanding rookie season, as did Knicks center Bill Cartwright. There was no doubt that Larry might have had a better year than the other two, but it seemed to be the unofficial opinion that he did the most to improve and help his team. After all, the Celts had gone from 29-53, to 61-21, and that was the greatest turnaround the league had seen.

One thing remained, however, the playoffs. Larry and his teammates wanted another world title. The media people loved it, too. The early favorites to make the finals were the Celtics and Lakers, and if that happened, it would be Larry Bird vs. Magic Johnson once again, just like in the NCAA finals of the year before.

The Celts hadn't been in the playoffs for two years, but because they won the division, they drew a bye in the first round. In the Conference semifinals, they had to face the Houston Rockets in a best of seven series, and they got off the same way they had in the regular season.

They made it look easy in game one as seven

players scored in double figures and the team won, 119-101. The second game was just as easy, a 95-75 laugher, as everything was balanced again. The team didn't need a big effort from Larry so he had just fifteen and fourteen in the first two games.

Game three also went to Boston, and in the fourth game the Celts really laid it on, winning 138-121, to eliminate the Rockets in four straight. Larry had 34 in that one, while Maxwell canned 27 and Carr 23. It certainly seemed as if the Celtics were headed for the title round, but they'd have to get past Philadelphia in the Eastern final.

The Sixers wouldn't be easy. They had their own superstar forward in Julius Erving, the spectacular Doctor J, who could break any game open when he got going. They were strong up front with 6-11 Darryl Dawkins and seven-footer Caldwell Jones. With Bobby Jones and Steve Mix coming off the bench, their front court seemed tough. Maurice Cheeks, Lionel Hollins, and Henry Bibby provided a veteran backcourt.

Boston Garden was the site of the first game, and the old arena was packed to the rafters with more than 15,000 fans screaming for their Celtics. They had plenty to cheer about in the first half as Boston took a 52-44 lead. But the Sixers stormed back behind Erving for a 16-2 burst in the third period that gave them the lead. Despite outstanding play from Larry and Cedric Maxwell, the Celtics couldn't catch up and Philly won in an upset, 96-93.

The key play came with the score 94-93, when the Doctor drove toward the hoop. Larry went with him, and Archibald dropped off his man to help. That left Henry Bibby open and Julius hit him for the winning hoop. Larry had 27, Maxwell 21, but the rest of the club couldn't balance it out to stop Philly's second half effort.

The second game went a lot better. Larry missed his first three shots, then erupted for 10 of his next 13, giving the Celts a lead they never relinquished. But when Larry sat down for a couple of minutes late in the first half, Philly ran off a 12-1 streak and almost caught up. But Larry then scored the first six points of the third quarter and his club was on the way again. They won it, 96-90, to tie the series.

Larry had scored 31 points, but said that nothing special was designed for him. "We just played the way we were supposed to play. We moved the ball to the open man and hit our shots. I was hot in the first half and the guys got me the ball."

Back in Philadelphia for game three, it was close for a half, Boston leading by two. But the Sixers erupted in the third period behind the Doctor again, and grabbed a 12-point lead into the final session.

Then the Celts began pecking away. When Larry and late-season acquisition Pete Maravich, hit three point plays, the Celtics pulled within two. But that's where they stalled. Philly won it, 99-97, to take a 2-1 lead. Despite being shadowed by defensive specialist Caldwell Jones, Larry managed 22 points in this one.

Game four was a crucial one. The Celts needed it to get even, and if they didn't get it, their backs would be up against the wall. They didn't get it. Philly again broke things open in the third period with a 17-5 burst that increased their lead to 16 and they coasted home with a 102-90 victory and an impressive 3-1 edge in the series. Larry had nineteen points to lead Boston, but it wasn't nearly enough. Suddenly, the Celtics looked as if they were headed for defeat, and definitely not at all like the balanced team of earlier in the season. One more loss and they were eliminated.

The teams returned to the Boston Garden for the fifth game, and there really weren't any exciting details to relate. The Sixers methodically destroyed the Celtics, almost making it look easy, leading by two at the quarter, six at the half, ten at the end of three, and a 105-94 final. Larry had his first real off game, scoring just twelve points as the Celtics' season came to an end.

Strangely enough, the Sixers won by playing better team ball than the Celts. For some reason, Fitch stayed basically with his starters, didn't use his bench, and began relying too much on just a few scorers. When angular Caldwell Jones began playing Larry in game three, he had difficulty getting inside and there just wasn't anyone to pick up the slack.

After the game, a discouraged Larry Bird talked to the press more than usual.

"I remember when I got here at the beginning," he recalled. "I was lost. I was more lost than anybody in the world. I didn't know what to expect. My first night helped because the fans gave me a standing ovation, and that made me relax. I was always treated well by the fans and I think I played as much for them as I did for the team.

"Overall, I think we had a good season. The toughest thing I felt was the length. We played all those games and at about midseason, I thought it is really a long year compared to college. But I was planning on it continuing. The other day someone called me from back home and I said, 'I'll see you about May 20, or so.' I thought we'd be playing until then."

So losing hurt, as it always does. But both Larry and the Celtics can be proud of their accomplishments in 1979–80. He can return to French Lick knowing that he is now totally appreciated as a basketball player. No more small school syndrome, lack of competition, can't run, can't jump, too slow for the pros.

In fact, many people thought the Rookie of the Year voting would be a toss-up between Larry and Magic Johnson, who turned out to be a champion again, winning the Playoff MVP prize as the Lakers won the title. Some even thought the Knicks' Bill Cartwright might sneak in. But when the voting came through, Larry Bird had won . . . and in a landslide over Johnson and Cartwright. That, in itself, showed that the voters realized just how much he had done for his team.

And who knows, maybe the writer in the *Boston Globe* has it correct. After watching Larry perform with the Celtics for most of the year, he said:

"He is a year away from being the best player in America."

Whether others agree or not, one thing is for sure. Larry Bird is going to try his hardest to make that statement come true.

MOSES MALONE

WHEN THE HOUSTON ROCKETS came into The Summit Arena for their 1979–80 home opener, the public address announcer began introducing the team members, one by one, to the cheering crowd. When he came to the tall man wearing number 24, he said:

"And now the NBA's Most Valuable Player, Moses Malone!"

The crowd cheered loud and long as the 6 ft. 10 in., 235-pound center ambled onto the court and began slapping hands with his teammates. Once the game with the Indiana Pacers began, Moses Malone was all over the court, doing the things he does so well, and hustling every minute. At the end, he had 44 points and 29 rebounds, imposing stats, and the Rockets had a victory. He seemed more than worthy of all the introduction he had received.

Yet after the game, he quietly went up to the P.A. announcer and politely requested that in the future he'd prefer to be introduced simply as Moses Malone, no more superlatives. He didn't want any special introductions, just the same treatment the rest of the starters received.

That's Moses Malone for you. Quiet and unassuming, he prefers to do his job without fuss and fanfare, and doesn't want any kind of special adulation that might make him seem above or better than his teammates. Yet the other members of the Rockets are well aware that the big guy has become their bread and butter.

"He finished last season as the MVP and he's starting this one the same way," said his backup, Dwight Jones, after the game. "I play against Moses in practice and against other centers during games, and I can definitely say I'd rather play against the other guys. There are some centers who are bigger than Moses and some who have better jump shots. But nobody—I mean nobody—has his overall game."

There are many who agree with Jones' assessment that Moses Malone is the best overall center in the game, the man you'd most want to have in the middle if you were starting your own team. But this opinion is shared mainly by players, coaches, writers, and ardent followers of the game. To the majority of average fans, the big names in the middle are still Abdul-Jabbar, Walton, Lanier, Cowens, Gilmore, Unseld.

Moses Malone is still not an everyday name among the superstars of the sports world. For one thing, he still has not played for a championship team, or a team that has come close to winning a title. For another, he has a low-key, introverted personality. He's not a troublemaker, or a publicity seeker. He doesn't try to be a "personality," a guy looking to make a name for himself off the court. He comes to work, does his job, and goes home. In fact, ex-teammate John Lucas described Mo's (his nickname) style by calling him "a blue-collar worker" among the other stars.

His coach, Del Harris, is another who has described Mo's low-key approach for those who can't figure the big guy out.

"Moses Malone has simple interests," says Harris. "He knows where he's going and the best way to get there. Mo isn't sidetracked by accolades or people who might want to be his friend just because he is a great basketball player."

Former Washington coach Dick Motta put it this way: "You can't knock what he does just because he doesn't audition to be a television commentator every day. You can win with him. That's the bottom line.

"He knows his limitations and his strengths. He has got everything reduced to its proper terms as far as his game goes. The scary part is his age. No one can envision his limits."

At the start of the 1980-81 season, Moses Malone will be just 25 years old, yet he will be going into his seventh full season as a pro. He goes into it almost unanimously acknowledged as the best rebounder in the game at both ends of the court. At the offensive end, according to experts, he has no peer in the entire long history of the game. Moses already holds every offensive rebounding record in the book.

But that's not all he can do. The past two seasons he has been the number four and number five best scorer in the NBA and in 1978-79, the league's

Most Valuable Player. In addition, he won the MVP prize with a team that tied for just the sixth best record in the league, a most unusual occurrence. The MVP almost always plays for a division winner or a title team.

Still, ask nearly any basketball fan about the big center who came directly from high school into the pro ranks and most will immediately mention the name of Darryl Dawkins, the 6 ft. 11 in. giant who plays for the Philadelphia 76ers. Darryl is always making news of one kind or another, and is often sought out for interviews by reporters.

It's his style, and he is becoming a top flight center. But the point is this: Dawkins indeed came into the NBA right out of high school and has been brought along slowly by the Sixers. It took nearly four years for him to become a starter, and his first season, 1975-76, he played in just 37 games and saw 165 minutes of action.

Moses Malone came right out of high school, also, a year earlier than Dawkins. But he didn't go to the NBA. Instead, he went to the ABA, a league without the stature and recognition of the older loop. Yet playing for a team called the Utah Stars, rookie Malone played in 83 games, saw 3,205 minutes of action, averaged 18.8 points a game, and corralled 1,209 rebounds. He did all this in what should have been his freshman year of college. Though just a handful of players have made this jump, it's hard to imagine a single one who could have produced these kinds of stats in similar circumstances.

Mo's coach that year with Utah was Bucky Buckwalter, who recalls what it was like at the beginning.

"Everyone knew Mo was young and a lot of guys really laid it on him, trying to intimidate him. There were elbows, knees, grabbing, shoving, the whole bit. But he gave it right back, didn't back up an inch.

"I knew it was going to be that way, so I told our guys to go after him right from the first day of practice. We had to find out how he'd react. They used to kid him all the time by calling him 'the rookie.' But one day after a real rough workout he walked into the locker room and announced, 'You guys can keep calling me a rookie, but I'm the toughest rookie you ever saw.' "

He was right. From the first he confounded the experts who said he'd be out of his element, a boy among men, that the pressure would get to him, and if that didn't, the grind of the long schedule would. Because he was shy and didn't say much, they figured he couldn't handle being on his own in the pros. Some even questioned his intellect because he preferred not to talk about most things. But Moses Malone always had two very important qualities, confidence and the ability to back it up.

The unfortunate part was that he joined the ABA at the time it was ready to fold. After playing one season for Utah, the team folded, and he found himself on another ABA team called the Spirit of St. Louis. An injury knocked him out for half a season, then the entire ABA went under.

He was put in a dispersal draft for the NBA and was picked by the Portland Trailblazers, who apparently didn't think he could play. The Blazers shipped him to Buffalo, and they didn't think he could play. After six games, the Braves sent him to Houston, and Moses had a home. By the end of the

1976–77 season he had an average of 13.5 points a game and had grabbed 1,072 rebounds. In what would have been his junior year at college, Moses Malone had shown he could successfully compete with the best basketball players in the world.

Through this entire odyssey, the young man from Petersburg, Virginia, showed again and again that he could live with and overcome tremendous pressure. He was such an outstanding and dominant player his final two years in high school that college recruiters from all over the country flocked to see him and attempt to woo him to their schools. Some said it was like guerilla warfare near his home, recruiters literally appearing from behind bushes, and out of alleyways.

Just when he began narrowing down the choices, the pros entered the picture. In fact, Mo had signed a letter of intent to attend the University of Maryland when the Utah Stars began plunking down the dollars.

When he finally made his decision, he had to prove himself all over again on the court. He wasn't eased into it as Dawkins was. He was thrown to the wolves and had to sink or swim on his own. Then, after two NBA teams showed absolutely no confidence in him, he had to go out and do it all over again at Houston.

All this speaks of a man of very strong character, a purposeful man, who came through a small-town upbringing with limited education, yet faced the realities of the world and never wavered. Moses is indeed an amazing man.

He was born in Petersburg on March 25, 1955, an only child. The odds of him ever growing into an NBA center must have been astronomical. His father was just 5 ft. 6 in. and his mother 5 ft. 2 in., both below average height, and when Moses was just a baby he was so very skinny his mother called him "Teeny."

There were problems very early in Mo's life, though he was probably too young to remember. His parents were having problems and when Moses was just two, his mother asked his father to leave. Mr. Malone did and from that point on, Mary Malone raised her son by herself.

She had been the eldest in a family of nine and had known hardship all her life. She was forced to leave school in the fifth grade to help support the rest of the family and had been working ever since. In fact, coming from a family of nine children, it must have been awfully easy for Mary Malone to raise one son.

Perhaps that's why she was bent on spoiling Mo. She figured he'd have it hard enough when he grew up, so why not try to make his childhood as pleasant as possible. Whenever she had a little extra money she would buy him something, a toy or an article of clothing, yet the old house they lived in on St. Matthews Street had faulty plumbing and a hole in one wall where a window should have been.

But she made things easy for her son, saying, "I didn't like him to work at all. I remembered how hard it was for me as a child and I didn't want him to have to live like that. He'd have to work hard enough later."

When Moses was just six, Mary Malone gave him a fancy toy organ for Christmas, sparking a lifelong interest in music which carries over to this day. Young Moses spent hours noodling around with the organ and it's still in his room at his mother's new house, a happy memory of his childhood.

Sports also became a big part of Mo's childhood. Football was the first game he was drawn to, but soon after he began playing basketball as well. He and his friends often played at the Virginia Avenue playground which was very close to his home. It's hard to know exactly what Moses was thinking in those days in terms of the future, but he certainly must have had the right instincts. When he was about 13 years old, he decided to forget about football and just concentrate on basketball.

An old friend of Mo's, David Pair, remembers how it was when Mo began playing a lot of hoop.

"When Mo first began playing on Virginia Avenue," Pair says, "he was still growing fast and he was very awkward. The other kids used to laugh at him and beat him all the time. But it wasn't too long before things changed and when the kids would play with Mo they make him agree not to come inside. He had to shoot from outside or they didn't let him play."

So the big guy was getting better in a hurry. He was well aware of his growing skills and when he was about 14, he did a very unusual thing. One of the few pieces of literature around his home was the family Bible, which his grandfather had passed down to his mother. Young Moses wrote a note one day and put it inside the Bible. The note was a promise to himself which said he would become the best high school player in the country by the time he finished his junior year.

With this definite and lofty goal in mind, Moses worked even harder, and he recalls becoming annoyed with some of the restrictions his friends in the neighborhood were putting on him.

"When I was 15, I was already 6 ft. 6 in." he says, "and the other kids at the playground would only let me play guard to take away my advantage under the boards. I couldn't even rebound and certainly couldn't improve inside. So I figured I had to have another place to play."

With the time Mo was putting in, he wanted to do it right. There was a nearby playground with coin-operated lights. A quarter bought an hour's worth of light. That was added incentive, because the losers had to pay for the next hour.

"About twenty guys would be there," Mo recalls, "and the games never stopped. Sometimes I got home at three or four in the morning, but my mother didn't worry because she knew exactly where I was and what I was doing."

Still, he longed for better competition, where he could play underneath. He found the competition in a rather unlikely place, Virginia State Prison, which was very near Petersburg. Moses and a few other boys would be allowed to come in once a week to play ball with the inmates.

"It was no big deal," he says now, "just a bunch of guys and some kids who wanted to play ball. In fact, they kind of looked out for us in there and we never felt in any danger. But I have to admit, when you walk through those halls and hear those gates slam shut behind you, it's a creepy feeling."

The games at the prison were rough, but that never bothered Moses at all. From the very beginning, he never shied away from contact, but rather welcomed it.

"When I was growing up I'd always try to play against guys bigger than me," he said. "They'd push me around and I'd push them back. We'd both get plenty of bruises, but I learned to love that kind of game."

At about this same time, Mo entered Petersburg High School. He was a freshman in the fall of 1970, and there was great anticipation because everyone pretty much knew of his ability. He was still growing and improving. The only question mark about his physical makeup were his hands. They were unusually small for a person his size. But that's something he has always had to compensate for. Even today, Mo can palm the ball, but just barely.

He began his career with the freshman team and totally dominated the court. Finally, in mid-season, he was called up to the varsity, and in his first game he scored 30 points to lead Petersburg to an upset victory over archrival Midlothian High. The Moses Malone saga had begun. From that point on, he did nothing but improve . . . and rapidly.

Off the court, he did run into some problems. He had difficulty in the classroom and difficulty expressing himself, which led to the later misconception that Moses wasn't too bright. But part of it was his background, which caused him to view schoolwork as something very intimidating. Robert "Pro" Hayes, an assistant basketball coach who was like a second father to Moses, was well aware of the problem.

"Mo was very self-conscious then," Hayes said. "He didn't want to risk being embarrassed, so even when he knew something, he'd say nothing."

Moses also had some problems with his teeth then, adding to his self-consciousness and causing him to talk even less. When he did speak, he usually kept his head down and didn't look the other person in the eye. Yet none of this bespoke of Mo's innate character. That was another story entirely, and Pro Hayes would rather speak of that side of the Malone he remembers.

"Moses was always very independent and very proud," says Hayes. "He never asked anyone for money and he surely could have used it then. He never would brag, either, even though he knew how good he was becoming. His mother did a very wonderful job with him, but I've known a lot of other kids like Moses, and a good, sacrificing mother is not always enough. It's tough for kids like Mo. A lot of them get depressed. No matter what they tell you they all want both a mother and a father so much. That kind of kid can go either way. There's no in-between. Mo went the right way. He became strong and independent."

He also became a very dominating ballplayer. By his junior year he was a monster in the middle who already had the uncanny knack of getting the rebound, especially at the offensive end where most rebounders don't excel. Petersburg was undefeated during Mo's junior year of 1972–73 and won the state championship. That's when all the hullabaloo started. Mo had been so dominating as a junior that the Petersburg High in West Virginia had the best prospect in the middle since Lew Alcindor (now Kareem Abdul-Jabbar), and Bill Walton. It wouldn't take long for college recruiters from all over the country to find their way to tiny Petersburg.

When Mo returned for his senior year and was better than ever, at his full height of 6 ft. 10 in., and weighing about 210 pounds, everybody wanted him. Once again he made the Petersburg team imposing and unbeatable. He would average 36 points and 20 rebounds for the season, and about ten blocked shots per game as well. Often times he had to get the ball on his own to score.

The reason was simple. Moses was just so dominant and powerful inside, that his teammates knew he'd get just about everything that came off the boards. So they rarely bothered to work the ball into him on offense. They just took their shots as they came and left him to clean up.

"One night they were all off and I got something like 45 rebounds," said Moses, laughing about the incident. Undoubtedly, he converted many of them to points.

Whatever the formula, it fully worked again. The Petersburg club was unbeaten, giving them a 50-0 record over two seasons. They repeated as State Champs, and Moses Malone was the toast of the high school basketball world.

He was an unanimous choice on the *Parade Magazine* High School All-America team, a team that boasted other future pros such as Mike Mitchell, Ken Carr, and Phil Ford. But it was Mo who was the main attraction as the recruiters continued to stream in and the list of promises Moses was hearing grew longer and longer. Mo has mixed emotions when he thinks back to that time.

"We have five hotels in Petersburg," he says, "and there was at least one recruiter in each of them all the time. Everytime I left my house, I saw these guys. Some of them just moved into hotels for the entire basketball season.

"After awhile, I spent my time trying to hide from them. But that wasn't easy. Everyone in town knew me and it's not easy to disappear when you're

6'-10". Sometimes I wouldn't come home until three or four in the morning in an attempt to avoid them, but someone would always be waiting in my front yard. They would call at all hours of the day and night. They even got my girl friend's number and called there when I wasn't home.

"A lot of that was pretty awful at the time. But for a guy who had lived a relatively quiet life, it was also exciting. I found I could handle the pressure and I actually relaxed and enjoyed much of it."

So Moses had his head together pretty well. And those recruiters who came to Petersburg thinking they were going to meet a big, dumb kid who they could easily sweet-talk, had another thing coming.

"Because I didn't say much, a lot of those guys came figuring they could run a game on me," Moses recalls. "There was one guy who came down and right away wanted me to sign something. I asked him what it was and he said really nothing, just a paper that would give me a grant-in-aid. I guess he didn't think I could read, but one look at it and I could see that it was a letter of intent to attend his school. I told him what I thought about that deal and sent him packing."

At the beginning of April, Moses traveled to nearby Landover, Maryland, to participate in the first annual McDonald's Capital Classic, a high school all-star game between the Washington Metro All-Stars, players from the Washington, D.C., area, and the U.S. All-Stars, a team of seniors from the remainder of the country. The purpose was to give the college coaches a good look at the best prospects in the land.

Despite the presence of some fine ballplayers, Moses remained the center of attention, the player most everyone, including the fans, wanted to see. The summer before, Mo had attended a basketball camp run by superscout Howard Garfinkel, a New Yorker whose judgement of players was highly respected. Said Garfinkel:

"Mo was the first kid who was bigger than the camp itself. He was the best we ever had!"

It was reported by then that more than 250 colleges had already contacted Moses in one way or another. Rumors were he was considering North Carolina, Maryland, Detroit, and Houston. But he wouldn't confirm or deny any of these things, and the rumors continued.

Moses arrived late because he was back in Petersburg taking some extra exams in an effort to get his grades up to a C average so he could qualify for an NCAA athletic scholarship. He had dropped algebra for art to help improve his grades. Whether this kind of practice is right or wrong, Mo was making an honest effort to do it on his own.

When Moses finally arrived, reporters began asking him the usual questions about his choice of a college and the things he'd seen on his visits to some dozen schools.

"I don't ask too many questions when I visit a place," he said. "I look around and let my eyes ask the questions and get the answers. I'm always asked what schools I'm considering, but I never tell them. What I really want is to go to a school where I can help the basketball program, really contribute, and get an education. I want to play for a team where I won't sit on the bench, and then I want to play pro ball. And the one thing that makes me mad through all this is when someone thinks they can buy me."

Moses said that some eight or ten schools had made promises which would be considered illegal under NCAA rules, but he would not identify them. One reporter remarked that his high school must have done a lot for him, and Mo answered in a way that showed he was very aware of the things going on around him.

"To tell the truth, Petersburg High isn't really doing anything for me, or the other guys on the team," he said. "We did get new uniforms last year, but we didn't get warm-up suits which the football team got. We've won fifty straight games and two state championships, yet the baseball team is treated better and I don't know when they last won a game.

"People don't think I know about these things, but the basketball team brought in about $40,000 this past year. We had nothing but sellouts, and the year before it was about $30,000. But we have a black coach and black players, and even at the banquet all I got was a certificate, no most valuable award or anything."

Moses seemed to be implying a double standard at the integrated school. Whether that was entirely true or not, it was obvious now that Moses had an awareness and sensitivity to his surroundings, and that he did think quite a bit about the things he had seen and done.

Because he had missed the practices, Mo didn't start the game, but played backup to Rick Robey (later a star with Kentucky and then the Boston Celtics). When he got in the game he was nervous and a bit tentative. His small hands betrayed him and he bobbled some passes and dribbled the ball off his foot once. He scored just eight points, but he did grab seventeen rebounds and blocked a few shots as his U.S. All-Star team won, 101–82. The MVP of the game was Butch Lee, who went on to become an all-American at Marquette. But the scouts and coaches still saw the awesome potential in Mo, and they wanted him more than ever.

After the Landover All-Star game, Moses returned home to finish the school year. Little did he know then, but the real drama had not yet begun. It seemed by this time the man who was making the biggest impression on Moses was Lefty Driesell, the dynamic and colorful coach from the University of Maryland.

There was an early report that Driesell had come on too strong, too quickly, and that Moses was turned off. But Maryland was always included in the various lists of schools that Mo was allegedly considering. Soon Mo was heard to say things like, "Lefty is the type of fellow who tells you things right." As it turns out, Maryland was always the big guy's first choice, though he kept this knowledge to himself, and the recruiters kept coming.

While all this was happening, a second scenerio was being played nearly across the country in the state of Utah. There was a franchise out there in the young American Basketball Association, the Utah Stars, and like the rest of the ABA, they weren't sure just where their future lay. The league had begun in 1967 as a rival of the established National Basketball Association, but by 1974, the ABA was on shaky grounds. Attendance was down, a number of franchises were in trouble, and some of the top stars were defecting to the NBA.

Several years earlier, the ABA had ended a long-standing unwritten rule by drafting college players who had not yet completed their undergraduate eligibility or whose classes had not yet graduated. To keep the pace, the NBA instituted its own "hardship" draft. So both leagues had loopholes under which to compete for top undergrads.

In April of 1974, the Utah Stars were prepared to go one step further. On the third round of the ABA draft they picked Moses Malone. They did it quietly and without much fanfare, and no one really took the pick seriously. Maybe the Stars were trying to establish the rights to Moses and could seriously pursue him in two or three years, once he had some big-time college experience under his belt.

Then events in Utah took a nose dive. The Stars' first pick in the 1974 draft was an undergraduate who decided to stay in school for another year. Their second round pick studied the situation and decided he'd be better signing with the NBA team that had picked him. Shortly afterward, the team was sold to a new group headed by a man named Jim Collier.

Collier thought it might be worth a try to get Malone. He already had a veteran center named Zelmo Beaty, who had been a great star in the NBA and had come to the ABA for a big price to finish his career. But Beaty was unhappy in Utah. Collier began negotiating to keep him there and the haggling dragged on into the summer.

Now it's back to Petersburg in late June. Moses Malone has graduated from high school with his necessary C average, and he has made his choice. This one did get a lot of publicity. Moses announced he had signed a letter of intent to attend the University of Maryland and play ball under Lefty Driesell.

So everything seemed set. Now it was just a matter of waiting the two months or so until Mo actually began attending classes at Maryland. Until then, it really wouldn't be totally official. And at that point, it can be safely said that Moses fully intended to go to Maryland with no thought of joining the pros.

Nothing changed until the final week of August approached. That's when the Utah Stars learned they couldn't re-sign Zelmo Beatty. He had decided to jump back to the NBA with the Los Angeles Lakers. When that happened, Jim Collier made a quick decision.

"Let's go get Malone," he told Player Personnel Director, Bucky Buckwalter and General Manager, Arnie Ferrin.

Collier meant it, and on August 22, the three men left for Petersburg. Moses and his mother were informed that they were coming by Dick Sadler, who was the manager of then heavyweight boxing champ George Foreman, and a part owner of the team.

"We decided to stay at a Holiday Inn, 15 miles north of Petersburg," Buckwalter remembers. "There were at least six toll booths between where we stayed and Malone's house. Arnie and Jim thought we'd sign Moses quickly and each had brought just two pairs of clean socks. I knew better. I brought enough for two weeks. And by the time we finished our business there we used some $92 in quarters for the tolls."

So the odyssey began. On Friday, August 23, Moses and his mother went with Buckwalter back to the Holiday Inn and for the first time big numbers were put in front of the young star, since the Utah brass had a contract right on the table. Once again Moses had a huge decision to make. Moses and Buckwalter agreed that Lefty Driesell ought to be informed on the new turn of events.

When he heard that Utah was after his prize recruit, Driesell himself came running to Petersburg, and he also called in Donald Dell, an attorney and former tennis professional who had represented a number of tennis players, including Arthur Ashe. Dell came in as an unofficial advisor, being careful not to violate the NCAA rules prohibiting college athletes from having lawyers or agents involved in any kind of negotiations with the pros.

Dell also called in one of his law partners, Lee Fentress, and the two went over the Utah contract. They then gathered Moses and his mother together and explained the loopholes in the contract. He also told Moses that Utah would undoubtedly be back to raise the ante if he didn't accept, and suggested the youngster call him for advice.

"A day later Moses called me eighteen times from Petersburg," Dell recalls. "Every time Utah made a new move he called. I knew then that he was a lot smarter than he was given credit for."

By now the story was front page, and the Utah people weren't about to quit. "It was unreal," recalls Buckwalter. "In six days we put more than nine hundred miles on the car just going between Petersburg and Washington. We had an outpost on a hill overlooking Moses' house. We'd drive up there, park the car, check the layout to see who was around, and then go in. One time we actually crawled through the backyard and were attacked by a big dog."

All these meetings served to firm up the offer, up the ante, and slowly close some of the so-called loopholes in the contract. Moses' mind was beginning to change, though his mother was undecided. The opportunity for him to get an education was an idea she could not easily shake.

One of the Maryland stars then was guard John Lucas, later a teammate of Mo's at Houston and now a member of the Golden State Warriors. Lucas had befriended Moses during his visits to the College Park campus and was also privy to the negotiation sessions. He began to see the change in Moses as Utah kept up its sales pitch.

"I really believe Moses knew what he was doing all along," said Lucas. "The more he heard, the more he wanted the pro atmosphere, all the looseness. Mo's nothing like he appears to be. He was already an extraordinary guy, way ahead of his time."

Finally on the following Wednesday, the day before he was supposed to start his first semester at Maryland, Moses went to Dell's office in Washington and told the two lawyers, "I've decided to turn pro. You can stop being my unofficial advisors and be my agents."

That did it. When informed of the decision, Driesell made one last effort to keep his prize catch and what he thought would be an instant national championship. He asked Moses to wait a year or two before making his decision, becoming very dramatic in the process and even making some references to the Bible.

The contract was on the table, but it couldn't be signed. There was a law in Washington stating that a person under 21 could not sign a document such as a pro basketball contract. So the entire troupe had to drive back to Virginia, where Moses finally signed the contract. He was now a pro.

Terms of the Utah agreement were never officially revealed, but estimates were that it was worth some $3 million spread out over a period of ten years. Of course, no one knew how solvent the Utah franchise and the entire ABA were, so there was a bit of a calculated gamble involved. And there was also the matter of Moses' age and inexperience. Could he compete as a pro? Even the ABA wasn't for kids.

"I knew people would say right away that I couldn't compete," Moses said. "But I told the Utah people right then and there, it didn't make any difference how old I was, because I still thought I could bust 'em. You just watch my action, I told them."

He told the same thing to the press when they questioned him. His confidence for a 19-year-old was amazing.

"I've seen the pros on TV and I figure I'm quicker," Moses said. "People talk about experience, but I never thought experience meant that much under the rack. I told my momma to let me decide. If I'm going to lose, let me lose myself. So she said all right."

The rack was Mo's term for the basket, where he figured he could operate against anyone. Others weren't so sure. Donald Dell, for one, said he couldn't sleep for three nights after the signing, wondering what was going to happen to Moses and thinking that "I really might be a flesh peddler."

Someone else who was thinking about it was Gerald Govan, a 32-year-old journeyman forward with the Stars. He, too, thought Moses might be headed for disaster.

"I started thinking about a high school kid being around a bunch of older guys and I had to wonder if he'd enjoy it," said Govan. "My wife and I discussed it quite a bit. Then I thought, maybe it won't bother him because in a way all of us older guys are really just kids playing a kids' game.

"When Moses came to camp he was a pleasant surprise. He's got a lot to learn, but right now he's as good as any college star coming in. The guys don't think of him as a 19-year-old kid, but as a player. That's a tribute to him and his ability."

One person who had no doubts that Moses' decision was right was veteran pro star Spencer Haywood, who years earlier had left the University of Detroit after two years to sign with the ABA, one of the first players to do that. Said Haywood:

"Look, the colleges are there just to use you. So if you're black and don't have rich parents, then you have no choice. You've got to take advantage of what you have as soon as you can."

But Moses was the one who would eventually have to decide his own fate. As Gerald Govan said, when he came to his first pro camp he fit in rather quickly. He was a hard worker, willing to learn, and equally willing to mix it up inside with anyone. His teammates must have been impressed when he told them they could call him a rookie, but he was the toughest rookie they ever saw.

Bucky Buckwalter, who had been elevated to coach after Mo's signing, was very impressed with the youngster's amazing speed.

"He's so quick it's unbelievable," Buckwalter said. "One minute he's just loping down the court, maybe just over the halfcourt line, and then you blink and he's coming down with a rebound. He stuns me sometimes. Here he is, a guy 6' 10", and he's as quick as a guard. Hell, he's quicker than a lot of guards."

The Stars would have preferred to ease Moses into the lineup, but frankly, the team needed his talent. In the team's first six games, Moses was on the court nearly 70 percent of the time. He quickly showed his instinct for the rebound, pulling down 65 in those six games, including 27 off the offensive board.

Unfortunately, Mo's contribution wasn't helping the team that much. The club won just one of its first six games, and some were quick to point out that a team couldn't expect to win with a kid barely out of high school in the lineup. But veteran Gerald Govan saw it differently.

"Moses has been amazing," said Govan. "People ask if all the money he supposedly got makes the older guys a little uptight. No way. It's really not right taking a kid out of high school like that. In a sense, he's being deprived of four more years of school and should be compensated for it.

"The bad part is the slow start the team has gotten. I've heard people refer to Moses as Super Baby, and blame him for the losses. That's not fair. We've lost Zelmo Beatty, Jimmy Jones, and Willie Wise. You just don't replace guys like that. Moses is doing a lot more than anyone expected. He's got a lot of poise. He's cool, maybe too cool. I hope he doesn't emulate the veterans too much. I think we overdo the super-cool thing. I'd like to see him hold onto some of that high school enthusiasm. It's refreshing around here."

Moses was playing it cool in another way, too. He was only doing the things he knew he could do on the court. He concentrated on getting the ball, because that was his big strength. When an opportunity to score in close, on a rebound, or layup, came along, he took it. He wasn't shooting from very far out and it didn't take the critics long to jump on that. But after six games he had 79 points for a 13 point average, and was the only player on the team shooting more than 50 percent from the field.

Despite the criticisms, he always maintained his composure, and told one reporter that he wasn't about to get rattled.

"I was never the kind of guy who let himself get nervous," he said. "I remember when we played the Nets. Everyone was asking me about Julius Erving and if I thought about playing against him before the game. Erving is certainly a great player, but I was thinking about me, not him, about what I wanted to do. All you can do out there is relax and that's my thing."

It was soon obvious that the Stars were not going to have a great year, but Moses seemed willing to make the most of the experience, as he continued to work hard in practice and in games, taking in everything his coaches and veteran teammates told him.

"He learns, boy does he learn," was the way Bucky Buckwalter put it.

Unfortunately, the Stars continued to have a difficult year. Midway through the season they brought in a new coach, Tom Nissalke, who Moses quickly grew to admire and respect. The rapport between the two helped ease the burden of Mo's rookie year.

"I was very homesick at the beginning," Mo admits. "But I kept my eyes open and a cool nead about things. I didn't pay attention to the things people said about me, didn't want to know what they were saying because I figured I was the only one who knew the truth."

When the league gathered for its annual All-Star Game early in 1975, Moses found himself playing on the West squad. Some thought his selection was more of a publicity stunt than anything else, but once again he showed he fully belonged. Playing just 20 of the 48 minutes, he scored six points and grabbed ten big rebounds, three of them off the offensive board. Projected over a full game, he would have had more than twenty rebounds against the best big men in the league. Moses belonged, all right, there was no doubt about it.

The Stars played better as a team the second half of the season, and while they didn't finish with a winning record, they nevertheless made the playoffs. Moses was a big part of their late-season surge, and he compiled some amazing statistics for a player in his position. It's hard to imagine any other player in the history of the game, with the possible exception of Wilt Chamberlain, who could have come into the pros from high school and done so well.

Playing in 83 of the team's 84 games, Moses was on the court for 3,205 minutes, an average of 38.6 a game. So, Mo was used even more toward the end of the season. He wound up with 1,557 points for an 18.8 average, shooting an outstanding 57.2 percent from the field, though most of his shots came from in close. He also corralled 1,209 rebounds, including 455 off the offensive board, best in the league. His rebounding average was 14.5 a game.

Utah lasted just six games into the playoffs

before being eliminated, but Moses played better than ever. He averaged 22.7 points, 17.5 rebounds in the six games, ending the season by serving notice that he was a player of awesome potential. He also seemed happy in Utah, with Nissalke as his coach.

Although there were very few black people in Utah, Moses didn't have any trouble adjusting to his life there. His high school was integrated and he always had white friends. Plus he kept to himself and was basically a homebody. As he himself said:

"I sit around, watch the scene, be quiet, and don't run my mouth off."

For a youngster of his age and experience, that seemed to be the right way to handle the situation. And as Moses had already shown so often, he always seemed to have the right instincts in different situations.

Though he had been a pro only a year, Moses had already won over a large number of his peers, the players and coaches. One of them was San Antonio coach Doug Moe, who told anyone in earshot that Mo was going to be a big star.

"I remember telling an NBA guy then that Mo was the greatest offensive rebounder I had ever seen," the Spurs' coach recalls. "Naturally, he didn't believe me. All the NBA people worshiped Paul Silas as an offensive rebounder, but he can't touch Malone."

Silas, a 6 ft. 7 in. forward, would later admit that he wasn't in Mo's class on the offensive board. "Mo has it down to a science," was the way Silas put it, "and offensive rebounding definitely is a science."

In the offseason Moses returned home and to the

new house he had purchased for his mother in the suburb of Ettrick. It was a ranch house, supposedly right on the route taken by Confederate General Robert E. Lee, when he made his final retreat through Petersburg before surrendering to Ulysses S. Grant at Appomattox, ending the Civil War.

Mary Malone loved her new home and was happy to have her son home for a while to share it with her. She was now sure they had made the right decision about the pros, especially when she heard how successful her son had been and saw what a good frame of mind he was in when he returned. She fully appreciated her new surroundings and told Moses that she often drove back to St. Matthews Street to look at the old place, which had been condemned after the Malones moved out. It remained a fitting monument to how far Mo had come.

It was back to Utah for 1975-76, amid new rumors that the ABA would be hard-pressed to survive another season. That didn't really bother Moses. Though he was happy in his present situation, he now had confidence in his ability and knew he could play somewhere. What he didn't know, was that in the next year, that confidence would be put to a brief, but severe test.

Before the regular season could begin, Moses ran into a problem. He broke the fibula bone in his leg and learned that he'd miss nearly half the year. This was a hard thing for an active kid like Mo to take. After all, basketball had been a constant part of his life for so long that the inactivity was difficult.

The problems were compounded when the Utah Stars folded before the season reached the halfway point. The team was no more and the players would be assigned to the six remaining ABA teams, which had been condensed into a single division in an attempt to last out the season. The ABA was about to die.

Moses was informed that he had been assigned to a team called the Spirit of St. Louis. Suddenly, he found himself in a new city, working to come back from an injury, and having to acquaint himself with new teammates, a new coach, and a new system. It couldn't have been an easy time for him. In a sense, he felt betrayed by the Utah people who had made all the promises. But with all the ABA franchises shaky, they couldn't really be blamed.

When he was finally ready to play he was still some fifteen to twenty pounds overweight and not in top shape. St. Louis Coach Rod Thorn began by using him at forward. The center was Caldwell Jones, who had come from another folded franchise, and the other forward was the talented, but unpredictable Marvin Barnes, who seemed to get in as much trouble off the court as he caused for opponents on it.

Out of his natural position and unsure of himself, Moses didn't approach the form he had shown as a rookie. His stats were down, he made mistakes and Thorn was only playing him about 27 minutes a game.

"You've got to remember he was just coming off an injury when he started playing for us," Thorn recalls. "So his production was off, but I always noticed the intense competitiveness in him and that led me to believe he would become a fine pro, though I must admit I never envisioned him an MVP."

"Moses played almost all forward for us, but every point he made came on tip-ins and offensive rebounds. He didn't seem to have much of a shot. His small hands also seemed to be a problem and he was involved in a lot of turnovers. I could see he was struggling, but he always had the discipline and determination to keep working and improving. He never dogged it for a minute or tried to take the easy way out."

Mo's two mates up front, Jones and Barnes, sort of headed up two factions among the team's players, and when Thorn saw the way Moses worked himself in, he was again impressed.

"By all standards, Moses was just a young, impressionable kid when he joined us," said Thorn. "It would have been an easy thing for him to start running around with Barnes' crowd and perhaps have gotten himself into trouble. But instead, he chose to hang around with Caldwell. I think that showed something about Moses' character."

And about the Malone instincts. He knew the situation in St. Louis with the ABA wasn't a good one, so he stayed in the background, watched and listened, and bided his time. He played in just 43 games that year, averaging 14.3 points and 9.6 rebounds, way off from his rookie year. But he got less playing time and was playing alongside two other very strong rebounders. His remarkable work on the offensive boards continued, however. Of his 413 rebounds, 196 came on the offensive boards, an incredible statistic to basketball purists.

When the season ended, Moses was again in limbo. It was officially announced that the ABA was folding, and that four of the six remaining teams would be taken into the NBA. They were Denver,

New York, Indiana, and San Antonio. The other two, St. Louis and Kentucky, would be disbanded, the players put into a special NBA draft pool. So for the third time in three years, Moses Malone would be going to a new team.

It was not the kind of pressure a kid who might just as easily have been going into his third year of college should have to endure. But Moses trusted his agents, Dell and Fentress, and he didn't panic. One of his biggest boosters through this entire period was his ex-Utah coach, Tom Nissalke, who had always taken a personal interest in Mo and kept in close contact with him.

"Mo was ready for the pros from the first day he put on a Utah uniform," said Nissalke. "He was never in over his head. I really believe that if he hadn't been hurt at the beginning of last season that Utah could have built their franchise around him and subsequently would have been one of the teams taken into the NBA."

That was a mighty endorsement, but unfortunately, "ifs" don't amount to much in the real world. Now he was in the flesh pool and waiting. The player most NBA teams were interested in was 7 ft. 2 in. center Artis Gilmore, who had played with Kentucky in the ABA. Already an established commodity, it was thought that Gilmore had the ability to turn a franchise around, and he was immediately tabbed by the Chicago Bulls, who had the first choice in the special draft.

Meanwhile, Mo's agents were trying to arrange a suitable deal, and they saw a good situation in New York, where the Knicks were still trying to fill a void in the middle left by the premature retirement of Willis Reed. New York might have gone for

Moses, but the club had recently been burned when they tried to sign star forward George McGinnis who decided to jump to the NBA. The Commissioner had voided that deal on a technicality and McGinnis wound up in Philadelphia. So the New Yorkers were hesitant to get involved in negotiations for another ABA player.

Unable to do anything behind the scenes, Moses and his representatives had to wait. Finally his name was called by the Portland Trailblazers, which had the number five pick. Portland might have been a good situation for Moses, but the Trailblazers had superstar Bill Walton, and if he could shake some persistent injuries, no one would move him out of the middle.

As it turned out, Portland had no intention of keeping Moses. They kept him through training camp and never gave him a full shot at making the club. Even in the exhibition season he was used sporadically, since all the time the club was trying to make a deal for him.

At one point, the Denver Nuggets almost bought him. They were an old ABA club and had seen him play, but the Nuggets' brass wasn't completely sold and finally opted for a proven veteran, picking up forward Paul Silas instead. Finally, just before the regular season was set to begin, Moses learned he had been purchased by the Buffalo Braves for cash and a draft pick.

So with the season opener just days away, he reported to Buffalo in a state of bewilderment about his future. But again, he followed the advice of Dell and Fentress, and his own instincts, and bided his time. The Braves had been a winning team in 1975–76, and the word was that they wanted a big center so they could move league scoring king Bob McAdoo to forward. Perhaps Mo would fill the bill.

But he never really had a chance. The coach at Buffalo was Tates Locke, who had tried to recruit Moses to Clemson when Mo picked Maryland. Perhaps that was in the back of his mind. At any rate, Locke decided to keep McAdoo in the middle and felt he was set at forward with John Shumate and Tom McMillen, Moses was second string.

There was also a rumor that the Buffalo people didn't consider Mo too bright (once again the result of him being so quiet) and didn't want to spend the time and effort to see if his career could be salvaged. The first week of the season Buffalo had two games. Moses played a total of six minutes, had one rebound and didn't score.

All the time, Fentress was working behind the scenes trying to pressure Buffalo into playing Mo or moving him. Old coach Tom Nissalke had taken over the reins of the Houston Rockets that year and when he heard Moses had gone to Portland, he suggested to team owner Ray Patterson that they buy him. But the Rockets were not on solid ground financially, and Patterson balked.

Now, with Moses obviously available again, Nissalke continued to pressure Patterson. Finally, the deal was made. Patterson agreed to buy Moses for cash and a couple of draft picks. It proved a lucky break for both Moses and the Rockets. The Buffalo situation continued to deteriorate. Before the season ended, McAdoo, McMillen, and Tates Locke were all gone. So Mo might have had real problems up there. Now he was in Houston, reunited with his old coach, and in a situation where he knew he was wanted.

"We were going down the tubes before we got Moses," Ray Patterson later admitted. "We wouldn't be in Houston today if Tom hadn't kept after me to make that deal. Moses made our franchise."

Everyone was relieved, including Robert "Pro" Hayes, Mo's old coach from high school. He had been following Mo's saga ever since he joined the pros.

"When Moses started to consider the pros I was really concerned for him," Hayes admitted. "I feared that if he was defeated he could really be destroyed, hurt for life. Since then, so much more has happened than we even imagined. First his team folded, then the league, then he was traded around so much in a short time. But through it all he remained Moses, the same Moses, not Billy Showboat. Apparently, Moses had a lot more faith in himself than we did."

In Houston, Moses was joining a team that had been an NBA expansion club in 1967-68, with the franchise starting in San Diego. Like most expansion teams, they were big losers at first, with one real superstar, Elvin Hayes, who joined them in 1968-69. Finally, in 1971-72, the team moved to Houston, where Hayes had been a college All-American, and they hoped to build a winner around the Big E. But before the 1972-73 season, Hayes had been traded to Baltimore and the club began all over again.

Prior to 1976-77, the closest the club had come to winning was in 1974-75, when they finished at 41-41. The next year they were 40-42, so they seemed on the brink of breaking through. The team Moses joined in 1976-77 had some fine potential and individual talents.

The heart of the team was its guards. Starting were 5 ft. 9 in. Calvin Murphy, an explosive scorer despite his small size, and rookie playmaker John Lucas, who had a great career at Maryland and who was already a friend of Mo's from the recruiting days. The third guard was rugged Mike Newlin, a tough 6 ft. 4 in. performer who played outstanding defense and scored in streaks.

Up front the club needed help. Rudy Tomjanovich was an outstanding shooter, but had deficiencies on defense and on the boards. The center was 7 ft. Kevin Kunnert, an average player at best who gave 100 percent but was neither an outstanding rebounder or scorer. The other front courtmen were mediocre players who might fill certain roles but no more. So there was a gap a mile wide which Moses filled right up.

Nissalke immediately installed Moses as starting forward opposite Rudy Tomjanovich, and let him go. Though he was officially a forward, he went to the boards constantly, often jumped center on tips, and sometimes guarded the opposing center when the matchups dictated it. It didn't take long for him to begin asserting himself.

The whole team began to jell under Nissalke. Mo's presence made a huge difference, allowing the club to gamble more on both offense and defense, because he was there to clean up underneath. From also-rans, the Rockets were suddenly battling the Washington Bullets for the Central Division lead.

Moses was again producing, just as he had with Utah his rookie year. He was an unselfish player and an extremely hard worker, both in practice and in games. He loved basketball and it showed, his enthusiasm for the game was contagious.

"Tom Nissalke has really utilized Mo's talents well," said rival coach Cotton Fitzsimmons. "He was Moses' coach in the early years and I think Mo respects him greatly. It's like Mo was just drifting until the two could get together again. He just plays his heart out for Tom."

Moses played extremely well down the homestretch, as did his teammates, and they won several key games that allowed them to take the Central Division crown by one game over Washington. Their 49–33 record was by far the best in the history of the franchise, and only three teams in the entire league had better marks.

As for Mo, he had put together an absolutely brilliant season. He was the club's third leading scorer behind Rudy Tomjanovich and Murphy, scoring 1,083 points for a 13.5 average. His 1,072 rebounds for a 13.1 average was the third best total in the league behind Bill Walton and Kareem Abdul-Jabbar. However, his 437 offensive rebounds were far and away the best in the NBA and set a new all-time league record. He also blocked 181 shots, seventh best in the league. He did all this playing just thirty minutes a game, as Nissalke didn't want to push him too hard and divided the playing time of all his players. Add another twelve or fourteen minutes and his stats might have been devastating.

The team was sky-high for the playoffs that year. They had a bye in the preliminary round, then went up against the Washington Bullets in the Eastern Conference semifinals. The first two games were played in Houston and the Bullets almost pulled off a double. They won the first, 111-101, and came within a hairsbreadth of the second. But Moses and his mates rallied to win in overtime, 124-118. Had the Bullets won, they might have carried the momentum into the conference finals.

But the OT win settled the Rockets down. They lost a close one in game three, 93-90, back at Washington, then evened it by winning, 107-103. A 123-115 victory back at Houston put them in a position to wrap it up back at Landover, Maryland, in game six.

Washington took the first half lead, 58-50, but the Rockets rallied in the third period to cut the margin to one, then came on very strong in the final session to win it, 108-103. They had done it in six games and were in the finals.

"We weren't too good in the first half today," Nissalke said, "but in the fourth period we really did some good things on defense and made it tough for them to score inside. Moses was just tremendous on the boards down the homestretch."

Mo retained a low profile through the entire series, preferring not to talk with reporters after the games. Again, it was his way. He had nothing against the writers, he just pleasantly declined interviews. There was plenty to think about, however. In the Eastern finals the Rockets would be meeting the powerful Philadelphia 76ers, a team picked by many to win it all.

The Sixers had super-forward Julius Erving and George McGinnis, Mo's old friend Caldwell Jones at center, and three fine guards in Doug Collins, Henry Bibby, and Lloyd Free. Darryl Dawkins, the other kid center who signed out of high school the year after Moses, played behind Jones and was getting increased court time. Steve Mix and Joe Bryant were fine backups at forward. The Sixers would be tough.

In the first half of the opening game at Philadelphia's Spectrum, Moses was a one-man team. He scored 22 points and grabbed eight rebounds, while the rest of the club floundered, Philly taking a 64–57 lead.

"Mo did exactly what we wanted of him in the first half," Nissalke said. "If he had gotten any help, we would have been in good shape."

Philly pulled away even further in the third period and then coasted home with a 128–117 victory. Moses finished with 32 points and twelve rebounds in a fine effort, while young Dawkins came off the bench to score 15 and grab 11 off the boards. The two youngsters had put on quite a show.

Game two saw the same pattern emerge, in that Philly had better balance and played stronger team ball, winning 106–97. They seemed like the superior team, and Nissalke confirmed that when he said, "Let me say that the 76ers simply have much more talent than us." Moses had only scored seven points in game two, but he led both clubs with eighteen rebounds. He was well on his way to acquiring his eventual nickname, The Chairman of the Boards.

But, of course, the important thing was getting a win, and back home at the Summit Arena, the Rockets did it, winning, 118–104, in a strong effort. This time Mo was devastating. He played 46 minutes, scored 30 points on 11 of 17 from the field, and eight of 16 from the line. Going up against the powerful Philly front line, he pulled down an amazing 25 rebounds. He was simply quicker and worked harder than his rivals.

A win in game four would have tied the series for the Rockets, but the club continued its spotty play. Caldwell Jones did a fine job denying Moses the ball, and from thirty points in the previous game, he scored just five. His teammates didn't seem to be able to work it inside. Once again Philly found the balance and won, 107-95.

Game five back in Philly should have ended it. With about four minutes left in the third period, the Sixers had a 17 point lead. But somehow the Rockets battled back. With seven players scoring in double figures, they managed to nip Philly at the wire, 118-115, with Moses getting 17 points and 19 rebounds. Now it was back to Houston for game six.

Houston had a two-point lead at the half, but some great play by Julius Erving enabled Philly to pull ahead in the third period. The Rockets tried, but they couldn't get the lead back and lost by a close, 112-109 margin. They had given the Sixers a good go, but were eliminated in six games.

In the finale, Moses had 17 points and 16 rebounds, and for both playoff series, the Bullets and Sixers, he averaged 18.8 points and 16.9 rebounds, both totals exceeding his season's output.

"Mo was absolutely great in the playoffs," said Tom Nissalke. "He did everything asked of him and more, and I don't think there's anyone around who doubts his ability any longer. When you think that this could have been his third year in college had he not turned pro, I would say his accomplishments have been amazing."

Even when it ended, Mo didn't say much for the

public. He was disappointed that the club didn't win and refused to talk about his own accomplishments in that light. With the public always looking for quotes and controversy from athletes, the silence regarding Moses made people still think he lacked brains and the ability to articulate. But as his good friend and teammate John Lucas said,

"When you're alone with Mo, you can't shut him up. And I'll tell you something else. He never forgets anything you tell him. In that way, he's almost like a book."

The Rockets came into the 1977–78 season with great expectations. One immediate drawback was that they hadn't really upgraded the team. The second-line players weren't really strong and the team lacked depth. But with the solid nucleus and hopefully even better Moses Malone, they thought they had a shot to get into the finals.

It didn't work that way, and the season can be summed up very quickly. In the team's 23rd game, a contest with the L.A. Lakers, a fight broke out between Kunnert and L.A. forward Kermit Washington. Rudy Tomjanovich rushed over to act as peacemaker, but all Washington saw was an enemy jersey rushing towards him. He turned and swung, hitting Rudy Tomjanovich on the button. It was a devastating punch in the face and Tomjanovich was finished for the season.

Shortly afterward, Moses broke a bone in his foot. He would miss some 23 games and then have to get in shape all over again. With the lack of depth, the club just collapsed, finishing last in the Central Division with a 28–54 mark. There would be no playoffs this time around.

While he was in there, however, Moses continued to show improvement. He was still playing mostly forward, though he was taking some shifts in the middle. In 59 games he scored 1,144 points for a 19.4 average, his best as a pro. He also grabbed 886 rebounds, good for a 15.0 average, which was second only to Truck Robinson's 15.7 norm. and despite missing 23 games he still led the league in offensive rebounds with 380. Even in his limited appearances and with a losing team, he was still a force.

Before the 1978-79 season, the Rockets made some major changes. Owner Patterson felt he needed a gate attraction after the disastrous 1977-78 season, so he took a gamble by trading his fine playmaking guard, John Lucas, to Golden State for aging superstar, forward Rick Barry. Barry was one of the all-time great players, an intelligent, high-scoring, all-around leader, but he was 34 years old with his best years behind him. To replace Lucas, the Rockets acquired another playmaker, Slick Watts from Seattle.

The other major move was the trading of Kevin Kunnert to San Diego. Patterson and Nissalke decided that center was Moses' natural position and they wanted the big guy to take over the middle on a full-time basis. Whether the acquisition of Barry was the right move is still a matter of conjecture, but the moving of Moses Malone into the pivot created a monster.

As soon as the season began, Moses began making his presence felt. Most of the league's players knew he was tough before, but given the freedom to do his thing and playing some 41 minutes a game had made him totally dominant.

His scoring average zoomed over twenty a game

right from the start and stayed there, and he was rebounding around seventeen a clip, far and away the best in the league. Barry, of course, did contribute some scoring, as well as his great court skills and leadership. Tomjanovich had recovered from his injuries and was again scoring around twenty a game, as was Calvin Murphy. So once again the Rockets began winning.

As the season continued, Moses began getting some accolades and national publicity for the first time in his career. It couldn't be helped. In every city in the league, writers and players were talking about Moses Malone, who in his first season as a regular center was often being called the best in the league.

"The people I've talked to all say that Moses Malone is playing the best center in the game," said Atlanta Coach Hubie Brown, "and from what I see I certainly can't disagree. Some say Kareem is the best and others say Artis Gilmore is the best. Both are exceptional players, but no one is playing better than Moses."

Brown's opinion was shared by many, because along with everything else, Moses was being tremendously consistent, keeping his game at a high level. During an eleven game stretch in January, he averaged 19.8 rebounds and 26 points while shooting 59 percent from the floor, and on some nights he was really out of sight.

On February 9, at New Orleans, he grabbed 37 rebounds, the highest total in the NBA since 1970, and 19 of those were off the offensive board. Nine days later against New Jersey he popped in 45 points. He was averaging nearly 25 a game and was among the top five scorers in the league. His fierce play was impressing everyone.

He worked so hard night after night that Elvin Hayes of the Bullets predicted he'd burn himself out by January 1. It didn't happen. He kept working.

"You can't change him," Nissalke said. "The last time he played against Kareem, he hung around practice for an extra half hour, having a ball, playing one-on-one. Then he goes out that night, plays fifty minutes in overtime, gets 25 rebounds and 34 points."

"I know how to pace myself," said Moses, when informed of Hayes' prediction. "All I know is after two or three quarters, other guys get tired and I just keep on coming. The bigger they are, the more I am a greyhound."

Washington's Mitch Kupchak was another convert to the fast growing Moses Malone Fan Club. "When you play against Moses you have to be looking for him every second," said Kupchak. "He's probably the most difficult guy for me to play, because he goes after everything, which means you can never relax. You have to keep boxing him out, making sure he doesn't sneak along the baseline."

Another center, Atlanta's Steve Hawes, put it this way: "It's very rare that you go into a game knowing that if you don't block out one man you're not going to win. But against Houston you know if you don't box out Moses Malone, and if he gets those 20 to 25 rebounds, you're most likely not going to win.

"He turns into an animal when he gets within five feet of the basket. He just refuses to concede anything, a rebound or a shot."

K.C. Coach Cotton Fitzsimmons said Moses' desire was the big thing. "He wants the ball and that's why he has no equal as an offensive rebounder," explained Fitzsimmons. "I've coached two great offensive rebounders in my pro career, Paul Silas and John Drew. They both wanted the ball, but not as badly as Moses does. It's his overwhelming desire that impresses me the most."

That desire is combined with hard work and homework. Moses finally took time out to explain some of the work that goes into his tremendous rebounding skills.

"Basically, I watch the flight of the ball, see where it's going, and try to get to that spot as quickly as I can," he said. "You can basically tell where it's going by where it hits on the rim and backboard. Most shooters in pro ball are going to hit the rim, and most of the good ones will hit the top of the rim. So you got to study the guys and learn how they shoot and know where the ball is likely to go when they miss.

"The good shooters will usually miss long, especially the ones who shoot those soft, arching also know if a player shoots a flat shot or a high archer.

"Of course, the guys you know the best are your teammates, so that gives you an advantage right there on offensive rebounding. For instance, I know that Rudy T. shoots a flat shot that will probably bounce back and Murf shoots with an arch, so I play the ball to come off a little differently."

Complicated business, this rebounding. But Paul Silas was right, Moses does have it down to a science. He had also learned to overcome the slight handicap caused by his unusually small hands. As one assistant coach said, Mo's hands are great above his head and going for the ball. "It was like he has magic in his fingers."

Teammate Mike Newlin added: "Mo's hands are like flypaper when he gets up there for a rebound, and he gets those arms out there quicker than any man I have ever seen."

With Mo playing so very well, the Rockets were battling San Antonio and Atlanta for the division lead, and the team was getting a reputation for coming behind in the fourth quarter. When that final twelve minutes began, other teams started running scared.

"That's because of Moses," said New Jersey Nets assistant Dave Wohl. "The man just never quits putting pressure on the player trying to block him out. If he's boxed out, he fights through. Or he darts to the left, or to the right. He's in constant motion until he gets a hand on the ball, and his man finally gets worn out fighting him all night. By the fourth quarter he's bushed, but not Moses. Once he smells that an opponent is weary, he goes in for the kill. And that's why the Rockets have been so good in the fourth quarter."

Rocket assistant coach Del Harris said the same basic thing, but a slightly different way.

"The one reason he's the game's best rebounder is that he goes after 150 rebounds a game," Harris explained. "His percentage isn't better than a lot of players, but he gets 20 of those 150, while other rebounders only go after 20 and get maybe five or six. Moses pursues a minimum of a hundred a game. He just won't forfeit any rebound unless it's a totally hopeless situation."

Moses himself seemed to relish his strong finishes and the fact that he had the ability to wear opponents down.

"When I'm moving no one can block me out consistently," he said. "And when there's a lot of contact and bumping around, I just get stronger. There's some guys who can block me out for two or three quarters, but I'm just waiting for that big quarter to come. I'm patient."

But with all the talk about his style and method of rebounding, it took Tom Nissalke to sum it all up in a way most people would understand.

"I think Mo's the greatest rebounder since Russel and Chamberlain," the coach said. "And he's only scratched the surface of his potential. I'd say he's only 60 percent of what he can be."

Whatever he was, he was plenty good enough to bring the Rockets back to prominence. The club finished with a 47–35 mark, a game behind San Antonio and a game ahead of Atlanta in what was a season-long dogfight. What a year it had been for Moses.

He led the league with 3,390 minutes played, scoring 2,031 points for a 24.8 average, tied for fourth best in the league. On the boards, he had no peer. He grabbed 1,444 rebounds, good for a 17.6 average, and he set an all-time record of 587 rebounds off the offensive board, getting some 250 more than his nearest rival.

Mo's great rebounding was made even more impressive by an interesting set of statistics which reach back into basketball's past. As good as Mo's 17.6 rebounding average was, some people took pleasure in pointing out that Bill Russell and Wilt Chamberlain used to average in the mid-20's.

However, it was pointed out that present day shooters are so much better that there are fewer rebounds to get.

When Bill Russell was in his heyday, the Celtics used to average some 80 rebounds a game. But in 1979, a typical rebounding team might get 45 or 50 rebounds at most. To be more precise, when Wilt Chamberlain averaged 27.2 rebounds a game in 1960–61, an NBA record, his Philadelphia Warrior team averaged 75.2 boards a game. But while Mo averaged 17.6, the Rockets as a team averaged just 45.3 rebounds. So the Warriors of 1961 had 66 percent more rebounds a game.

Broken down still further, it reveals that Moses grabbed 39 percent of his club's rebounds, and had he gotten that many for Wilt's Warriors, he would have averaged 29.3 rebounds a game. It was the highest ratio of team rebounds ever, breaking Wilt's record of 36.3 percent which he garnered with the San Francisco Warriors in 1962–63. So Mo's 1978–79 season may have been the greatest rebounding performance of all time.

He was rewarded, of course, with the Most Valuable Player prize after the season ended, but he still had one big disappointment. The team went nowhere in the playoffs. In the preliminary round they lost two straight to the Hawks, 109–106 at Houston, and 100–91 at Atlanta. You couldn't fault Moses. He averaged 24.5 points and 20.5 rebounds in the two games. It was still obvious that the Rockets did not have a balanced, all-around team.

There was another matter to attend to after the season. Mo's salary had been going up consistently and he was reportedly earning upwards of $800,000 a year, an incredible sum. Yet his pact was going to run out at the end of 1979–80, and he had already mentioned that he wouldn't mind playing with the Bullets, which would put him nearer his home in Petersburg.

Perhaps Mo was a bit upset with the Rockets' failure to build a strong team around him. As one writer put it, "Surround Malone with the proper players and not even Kareem Abdul-Jabbar could prevent him from hoarding titles the way he presently collects rebounds and points."

Moses himself was well aware, as he usually is, that he was now more than just a rebounder.

"I've always been a player," he said. "People just talk about my rebounding, but I don't buy that, no way. I'm a player and a scorer. Why don't they talk about my scoring, too? I feel I can do it all now, whatever I have to. But all most people see is my rebounding."

The Rockets certainly didn't want to lose him. New owner George Maloof made Moses his first order of business. In July, a new contract was announced, extending the old one through the 1981–82 season. No one knew the exact terms, but rumors had it that he would be earning more than $1 million dollars a year.

"I'm very pleased with the contract extension," Moses said. "I'll still be working hard, doing the best I can. Now I hope to play out my career here and make Houston my home."

So that was settled. One thing did upset Moses, Tom Nissalke would not be returning for the 1979–80 season. Del Harris would be taking over the team, but since he was an assistant, Mo already knew and liked him. The transition wouldn't be too difficult.

Houston did make some personnel moves, but

not tremendous ones. They brought in veteran center Billy Paultz to give Moses a capable backup. Guard Thomas Henderson was signed as a playmaker, perhaps the playmaker they hadn't had since Lucas left in the Barry deal. Rookie Alan Leavell also figured to get a shot at the playmaking guard spot. Murphy and Tomjanovich were back, as was swingman Robert Reid, who joined the team in 1977 and had contributed. But the balance that makes a champion was still missing, and it was evident from the start, when the Rockets played .500 ball but couldn't seem to get much above it.

Moses was having another outstanding year, though not quite as spectacular in the rebounding department. Perhaps the pressure of having to do so much was getting to him. When the season ended, the Rockets were a disappointing 41–41, tied for second behind Atlanta. They were in the playoffs, but couldn't realistically expect to go very far.

As for Moses, he had a career high 2,119 points in 82 games for a 25.8 average, fifth best in the league. He had 20 point support from Calvin Murphy, but Tomjanovich slumped to 14.2. In addition, he lost his rebound crown to Swen Nater of San Diego, who got 15.0 a game. Moses corralled 1,190 for a 14.5 average and second place. But there was no denying his skills. He was one of the best.

In the playoffs, the Rockets pulled a mild surprise by upsetting San Antonio in the preliminary round, winning the best of three series in three games. Moses was hampered by a bad ankle in the early games, but he came back to score 37 points and grab 20 rebounds as the Rockets won the deciding contest easily, 141-120. He was still at his best in the big games.

The only problem now was that the Rockets had to go up against the Boston Celtics in a best of seven series. The Celtics had the league's best mark in the regular season and were 6-0 against Houston.

Yet there was always hope. Moses said, "I don't want an early vacation. Even though they were 6-0 against us, I think we can beat them. I know I love to win and love to play the game hard. When it gets down to the main game, I'm gonna play."

Moses played, all right, but his club was just no match for Larry Bird, Dave Cowens, Tiny Archibald, Cedric Maxwell, Chris Ford, and the rest of the Celtics. Boston took the Rockets in four straight, maintaining their unbeaten string against them. Mo tried his best, including a 28-point effort in the final game when he got little support and the Celts won easily, 100-81.

Despite the tender ankle, he had a 25.9 average in seven playoff games, and grabbed 97 rebounds. But the loss was again a disappointment to a great season.

Today, Moses Malone is more confident and self-assured than ever, yet he still lives a quiet, relatively simple life, and he still loves the sport he plays so well. He will talk about himself a bit more now, stating the facts without sounding boastful, as has always been his style.

"Nobody ever taught me how to play this game," he says. "I taught myself when I was growing up by practicing hard and watching NBA players on television. It all came down to God-given talent and the pride that I have.

"I could play around the rack when I came into

the ABA, too. It was just that I never really got to chance to show myself until I came to Houston."

He has shown himself now, all right, and should continue to do so for a long time. After all, if Moses had taken the conventional route to the NBA, via college, he'd just be coming into his second pro season. Instead he's coming into his sixth, and he seems to be getting close to the top of his game. Teammate Rick Barry, who has seen a lot of great ones, says this about Mo:

"Nobody has played the center spot like him. Moses is unique. No one has ever had that kind of quickness for a guy his size. Without question, he's proven he's the best offensive rebounder in the history of the game."

Perhaps, though, it was old friend John Lucas who summed it up best, describing Mo and at the same time sounding a warning to the NBA. Said Lucas:

"Moses is just a *T* away from being *GREAT*. And when he gets that final letter, everybody just better watch out."

EARVIN "MAGIC" JOHNSON

WHEN HE WAS IN COLLEGE and the scouts broke his skills down, one by one, the picture was not of a potential superstar. They said he was just a mediocre shooter. He got off his feet, but was by no means a real leaper. On defense, they said he might be a step or two slow, and have difficulty guarding smaller, quicker opponents. In fact, if you didn't know his name, you might think he was destined to be a low draft choice or wasn't a pro prospect at all.

But just drop the name and everything changes. Earvin "Magic" Johnson! Hear that once and then tear up the scouting reports. Though the individual evaluations might be true, they mean nothing, for the man they call "Magic" is one of the most exciting court performers in the game today, and if you want to substitute something for his alleged mediocre shooting, average jumping ability, and possible defensive deficiencies, you can add this one liner—the man's a winner!

As a matter of fact, you can't be much more of a winner than Magic Johnson. In just a little over a year, he led his college team to the NCAA championship and was the tournament's Most Valuable Player, and then he turned pro and promptly led his pro team to the NBA title and in the process was named Most Valuable Player in the playoffs. It was an incredible "double."

Through it all, Magic Johnson exuded calm and confidence, a broad smile, and a perpetual sense of excitement and fun. He never rattled, never lost his cool amid the court pressure and a year-long publicity blitz that had his name in the news almost constantly. Whenever a game was on the line, college or pro, the Magic-man quickly showed he had come to play.

Of course, those scouting reports that said Magic couldn't shoot or jump that well, and might be a trifle slow, don't tell the whole story. Obviously, there are positive aspects, and plenty of them. For one thing, Magic Johnson stands 6 ft. 8½ ins. tall and plays guard! That's right, he's essentially a backcourtman, who handles the ball as well as or better than guards much smaller than he. When he joined the Los Angeles Lakers after a two-year stint at Michigan State University, he was billed immediately as the tallest point guard in NBA history.

As a 6 ft. 8½ in. point guard, Magic Johnson has an all-encompassing court presence. He sees the game as a whole, his vision taking in everything at once. When he began playing for Michigan State as a freshman, he helped turn the team around, not with his scoring, but with his passing. The Magic-man is just that when it comes to delivering the ball. He can make the great pass, the impossible pass, and that's a commodity that has been missing from the pro game for some time.

"The only one he makes me think of is Bob Cousy," said former NBA guard Bill Sharman, who was a teammate of Bob Cousy, the Celtic great widely considered the measuring stick for evaluating passers. "Magic is adventurous like Bob was. He's got great ideas and he's willing to try things. And, of course, he's so much bigger than Bob. I really don't think there's ever been anyone quite like him."

Sharman, of course, had a vested interest, since as General Manager of the Lakers, he made Magic the number one draft pick of the NBA in 1979-80.

"We knew what a great passer he was when we drafted him," Sharman continued, "but he turned out to be a much better shooter and rebounder than we thought."

Strike one criticism. The Magic-man actually shot better in the pros than he did in college. It must be remembered that he turned pro after his sophomore year at Michigan State, so he was still very young and improving. Then there was the charge that he wasn't a great leaper. With his size and skills he doesn't have to be. In fact, as an NBA rookie he was not only the best rebounding guard in the league, but the second best rebounder on his team behind 7 ft. 2 in. center, Kareem Abdul-Jabbar.

Defensively, he did make mistakes, rookie mistakes, but he showed great quickness for a man his size, and compensated in other ways if smaller guards were quicker. In fact, he proved tremendously versatile to the Lakers, moving up to the forward slot on numerous occasions and showing the ability to do the job at both the power and small forward slots.

And to top it all off, when Abdul-Jabbar was injured and couldn't play in the sixth game of the championship series against the Philadelphia 76ers, it was Magic who was moved into the middle and produced one of the greatest individual efforts in NBA playoff history.

So many things happened to Magic Johnson in the space of a year that it would be hard to imagine him as basically unchanged. But it's true. He has acquired none of the superstar syndrome, the hey-look-at-me-I'm-great attitude that affects so many of today's athletes. Outgoing, friendly, with a quick smile, secure with a small group of loyal friends, family, and advisors, Magic Johnson has met sudden and dramatic success head on, and with no change in his basic philosophical outlook.

"I'm going to keep on smiling because that's how I live," he has said. "When I get up in the morning I'm grateful to see the sun. And I'm going to be careful about how I come across to people. I don't want them to think I'm conceited. When you're the main attraction, you've got to watch out."

So far, Magic has lived by his rules. Playing in Los Angeles, in sunny California, and so near the make-believe world of Hollywood, it would be easy to succumb to the celebrity life-style. But while Magic has had many doors opened to him, he's been careful not to venture too far inside. Basketball and his team has always come first and that's the way it'll always be.

In a sense, Magic had been preparing himself for

all that has happened for a long time. Both his athletic and personal roots run deep, with strong and good influences all along the way. He was born in Lansing, Michigan, on August 14, 1959, the youngest of ten children born to Earvin Johnson, Sr., and Christine Johnson, the cornerstones of the large family and the two people most responsible for giving Earvin, Jr., the strength of character that has helped take him so far so soon.

Earvin, Sr., came to Michigan from Mississippi in order to find a better job for himself. He had played a lot of basketball before coming North, and he knew the game well, but once he arrived in Lansing he went to work and soon was supporting a growing family. That ended his playing days, but he continued to follow the game which later proved to be a great help to his son.

As a provider, Earvin Johnson, Sr., was a superstar in his own right. For some 23 years now, he has worked as a night man at the Fisher Body auto plant in Lansing, and when he needed more money, he took day jobs to get it. A big, impressive looking man of 6 ft. 4 ins. tall, Earvin, Sr., has always played a major role in his son's life, and the younger Johnson has never resented his father for a minute.

"My father always hoped his children would do something in life," relates Magic. "He didn't want me to have to join him, hammering auto bodies. He wanted something better for me, and for the others."

Christine Johnson also played basketball as a youngster in North Carolina, so Magic got the genes from both sides of the family. She, too, came to Michigan where she met Magic's father, married him, and started their family. Mrs. Johnson was also ready to contribute all her energies to the family. Besides taking care of the kids, she worked as a supervisor in a school cafeteria, and as with his father, whenever Magic talks of his mother it's with fondness and love.

"My mother often appears shy in front of strangers. But she likes to have fun and loves to talk, and I inherited that from her."

As to the sacrifices his parents made, Magic is well aware of them, as undoubtedly are all the Johnson children.

"If we wanted something, they always managed to get it for us," Magic says. "And the result of that was they didn't get much for themselves."

Magic began playing ball early. Basketball is *the* game in many Michigan cities, and the various playgrounds are usually crowded with youngsters playing the roundball game. At first, Magic played with his older brother, Larry. The two used to get up early Sunday mornings and go over to the Main Street School before other kids got there. They'd play one-on-one games, full court, and Magic says that's when he learned to dribble, because Larry would press him all over the place, from one end of the court to the other.

When he was in the fourth grade he began playing with other youngsters. One of his new friends was Jay Vincent. The two boys met and played together many times. Their friendship would endure right up to the time they both enrolled at Michigan State years later, Vincent as a 6 ft. 8 in. center and Magic as a 6 ft. 8 in. guard.

With his new friends and increasing interest in basketball, the Sunday morning sessions became even more important, even when brother Larry didn't go anymore. Christine Johnson remembers that Magic worked hard at his game, even then, taking it very seriously.

"We'd all be asleep when Earvin would get up and quietly leave the house to play ball," she recalls. "When he first started doing it I'd worry a bit and always ask him where he'd been when he got home. He'd always tell me the same thing, that he was up at the basketball court, playing ball. So I finally told him that he shouldn't ever leave home without letting someone know where he was. After that, for years, he'd wake me up at daybreak, every Sunday morning, to say goodbye and tell me he was going up to the court."

While he was growing up and even beyond that to this day, Magic has always had good and loyal friends. His fifth grade teacher was a woman named Greta Dart, and when she learned that Magic and some of his friends loved to play ball but couldn't get into the school gym without a supervisor, she recruited her husband for the job. So Jim Dart became Magic's first coach, and before long the Darts became his friends, people who cared about his welfare and his future.

It wasn't long before basketball was Magic's passion. He even went outdoors in the winter, often shoveling snow off the courts so he could get in some practice, or play a few three-on-threes with his friends. In the summer, he played until dark, when he couldn't see the hoop anymore. If no one else was around, he just practiced alone. Otherwise, it was one-on-one, three-on-three, or full court, whatever he could get.

And while he was practicing the fundamentals,

he was learning the technical aspects of the game from his father. Whenever they could, Johnson senior and junior would watch NBA games on television together. Magic would concentrate on the set as his father analyzed the game and explained what the players were doing and why, pointing out both the good and bad things he saw. This kind of private coaching gave Magic an early court sophistication that his peers didn't have.

"My father would point out things to me like Oscar (Robertson) taking a smaller guard underneath, or showing me how they ran a pick and roll," recalls Magic. "So when I started playing organized ball, if the coach asked if anyone knew how to run a three-man weave or shoot a left-handed lay-up, I was always the first one up."

As the boys got older, the games at the Main Street School became more intense. There were eight-foot high baskets there, so the boys could operate easier, and that's when Magic began using what he refers to as his "hoopsy doopsy" style of play.

"The place was often packed with kids and everyone wanted to play," he says. "The only way you could hold the court was to keep winning, the losers got off and had to wait their turn again. So we learned early that it was a lot better to go to the hoop on drives and get the sure two points, rather than lay back and pop pretty jumpers."

Magic also learned a lesson in those days which carried over and characterized his game right through high school, college, and into the pros. It was his sense of teamwork, and this, too, came out of the Main Street playground.

"I'd get to the playground and usually be picked

for a team right away," he remembers. "But I'd always ask the guy who else he had. And if he said he had a couple of real big scorers, I'd turn him down and wait for a guy who picked me but still didn't have any others. Then I'd tell him to get so-and-so, who was a good rebounder and so-and-so who was a good defensive player. That would make a good mix and I knew we'd have a *team*.

"If you had all the big scorers and one-on-one players, then the game breaks down. Before you know it, everyone is mad because one guy is showing off for a girl or another is trying to prove he's the best shooter from 25-feet out. But the team that played together always won, and my team won all the time."

It's unusual for so young a player to have this kind of team concept, but Magic knew where he was going and how to get there. He wanted to keep the court and to do that he had to win. He learned very quickly what it took to do that.

When Magic was in the eighth grade he was already about 6 ft. 3 ins. tall, but very thin and going through that awkward stage that didn't always show him at his best. He was playing junior high ball then and that's when George Fox saw him for the first time. Fox was the coach at Everett High School and would often go around to the junior high games to see what kind of players he had coming up.

"The first time I saw him he had a bad night. He seemed to be standing around a lot and taking outside shots. Then one day soon afterward, one of his brothers came up to me and said that Earvin wanted me to come to the game because he was going to set a junior high scoring record. So I went, and wouldn't you know it, he set a record."

That summer, Magic met Terry Furlow, who was getting ready to start his freshman year at Michigan State. Furlow liked the youngster and began letting him get into faster games. Before long, Magic was playing with Furlow and other top players from the Detroit and Lansing areas, some of whom were already pros. Besides Furlow, Magic played with and against the likes of George Gervin, Campy Russell, and Ben Poquette. It was quite an education for him, and when he returned to junior high he had improved as a player.

He was 6 ft. 4 ins. tall by then and filling out. He had a good year, but his true potential still wasn't quite showing. As George Fox said, "We knew we had a good player coming, but no sensation."

Fox would be another good friend to Magic in the coming years. As a coach, he wasn't a soft touch, and even had thrown one of Magic's brothers off his team for missing a practice during Christmas vacation. But once he had Magic, he took a personal interest.

"Magic was like a big kid then, and I wanted to make sure nobody hurt him. His family really meant a lot to me, also. If they had been wheeler-dealer types I wouldn't have cared, but they were totally decent people who wanted the best for their son."

Actually, Magic almost didn't go to Everett High. There was a busing problem in Lansing back in 1974 and under ordinary conditions, he would have gone to Sexton High, which was a predominantly black school on the west side of town near the Fisher plant where his father worked. But because of the busing situation, he was assigned to

Everett, which was considered a white school then.

In the two years before Magic arrived at Everett, George Fox had less than mediocre teams, finishing with 9-11 and 11-12 slates in those seasons. Then along came Magic and things began to change. But before he began playing for Everett his sophomore year, there were some problems to be ironed out.

First of all, Magic and some of the other black kids weren't too happy about being bussed to Everett. In addition, racial tensions sometimes ran high at the school, which didn't always make for a pleasant experience on a day-to-day basis. Then there was the incident a few years before when Coach Fox had kicked Magic's brother off the team. All that served to make Magic a bit apprehensive about playing there. That's when another person came along who was to give Magic advice and direction, and who became a long-term, loyal, and helpful friend.

Dr. Charles Tucker was a psychological consultant to the Lansing schools, as well as a former ballplayer. He had played college ball at Western Michigan and later had tryouts with several old ABA teams, including the Memphis Tams and San Antonio Spurs. So he knew a number of professional ballplayers and had an especially good rapport with athletes.

"One reason many ballplayers look up to me is that when I was cut by the Spurs, I went right back to school and got my degree," Dr. Tucker said, candidly.

Since he still enjoyed working out, Dr. Tucker would often play with the boys on the Everett team, as well as at other schools in the area. So he knew Magic and soon had his confidence. When he saw the dilemma that Magic and some of the other black ballplayers were having at Everett, he stepped in and gave them some advice. He told them not to dwell on the racial stuff that was going on and that Fox was a good basketball coach who would make ballplayers out of them.

So Magic and his friends began playing. His sophomore year he started, along with another black player and three whites. Many people say that the togetherness of the basketball team, along with Magic's bubbling personality, helped ease the tensions at Everett to the point that by Magic's senior year they were pretty much gone.

It didn't hurt, either, that the team was winning and winning big. The team rolled to a 22-2 record and went all the way to the Class A quarterfinals in the state tournament before losing, when they missed five one-on-one opportunities in the closing minutes. But Magic was already a force, making all-state as a sophomore and showing the great ballhandling, passing, and leadership qualities that would soon make him the object of many college recruiters.

That sophomore season also saw him acquire the nickname that would someday become a household word among sports fans. The man who gave him the name was Fred Stabley, Jr., a young sportswriter who was covering the high school basketball scene for the Lansing *State Journal*. Stabley recalls watching Magic for the first time.

"Everett opened against Holt High that year. Holt wasn't a very good team, yet they hung in there and Everett won by just one point. Earvin must have been about 6'-5" or 6'-6" then, and he didn't have a particularly good game. I'd say he was just average, nothing to really get excited about. Then I went to the next game and I couldn't believe my eyes. Earvin was incredible. He had something like 36 points, 18 rebounds, five steals, and 14 assists. And this was against one of the best teams in the area, Jackson Parkside High.

"After the game I went into the locker room and told Earvin he was something else. Then I figured he had to have a nickname that we had to call him something besides Earvin. Well, Dr. J and the Big E were both taken, and suddenly I said, 'How about Magic?' He said that was okay with him, so from that point on, he was Magic Johnson and it really caught on."

The next year the team was outstanding again. This time they were 24-2 for the season, but were disappointed when they lost in the semi-finals of the state tourney. Yet for Magic it was another banner year. An all-stater once again, he was still growing and dominating the games even more. Yet he never lost his sense of team play and rarely tried to do it all by himself.

Magic was on fire when the 1976-77 season began. He had his Everett team rolling and the scoring better than ever, using his height, speed, and driving ability to the fullest advantage. In fact, he was doing so well that it had George Fox worried. He wanted to be sure his club didn't turn into a one-man team.

"After our first four games that year, Earvin was averaging something like 44 or 45 points a game," Fox recalls, "but as a team, I didn't feel we were playing good ball. So I told him, 'Earvin, if you want to win the states, I think you'd better average about 23.' He simply said he understood and I never had to say another word to him. I think he averaged 23.8 that season. In a way, it was almost like he had it programmed."

That was still another aspect of Magic's game and personality. He was extremely coachable, a quality that's absolutely necessary for a team leader. So the team continued to win, as Magic attracted more attention as a future star. The thought of a kid that big who could handle the ball like a small guard had the college coaches tossing in their sleep.

Besides a balanced offense, the Everett High team also played good defense, thanks again to their coach. "Some teams just liked to trade baskets," George Fox said. "Not ours. We had pride in our defense and I'd always tell them not to give a club easy lay-ups. A lot of times we'd give clubs the baseline, because Earvin was so good at coming back and blocking their shots. Then away we'd go."

Everett went plenty that year. The club finished the year with a 27-1 record, but more importantly, finally took that elusive state championship. Magic, of course, was an all-state selection for the third straight year and he knew that he'd soon have a very big decision to make.

It had certainly been a great high school career for him. In one game his senior year he exploded for 54 points, and in his very next contest he handed out sixteen assists. Another time, when Everett was playing archrival Eastern High, led by Magic's boyhood friend, Jay Vincent, some 9,886 fans came to Michigan State's Jenison Field House to see the game, which was also on local television, where it drew a rating just a bit lower than the NFL Super Bowl had drawn from the Lansing area a couple of months earlier.

Naturally, all kinds of schools were after him and fortunately, Magic was once again surrounded by friends and advisors who had only his best interests at heart. Magic wasn't protected in the sense that he was sheltered, but there was no way recruiters were about to pressure or harass him, not with his father, Coach Fox, and Dr. Charles Tucker constantly acting as buffers.

It didn't take long for Magic to narrow his possible choices down to a select few, and as expected they were all pretty big name basketball schools, the likes of UCLA, Maryland, North Carolina, Purdue, Indiana, Michigan, and Michigan State. Of those schools, the least known basketballwise, was Michigan State. But the Spartans had one advantage. They were more of less Magic's hometown school, with the Michigan State campus located in nearby East Lansing.

In fact, if there was pressure of any kind on Magic it was to stay home and play for one of the Michigan schools. He had been the first three-time allstate highschooler in Michigan history, and there was tremendous interest and excitement in his future. Then Jay Vincent from Eastern High announced that he was going to Michigan State, and Spartan fans had visions of getting the two best schoolboy players in the state the same year.

Most of Magic's family and friends wanted him to stay close to home, and at first it seemed that Michigan had the edge. The Wolverines had the more successful program the past few years and had a well-known and dynamic coach in Johnny

Orr, who wanted Magic very badly, telling George Fox, "I would do anything to get that kid."

On the other hand, Michigan State's Jud Heathcote had only been at his present job a couple of years and had still not turned the program around, his record the past two seasons having been 14-13 and 10-17. Before he arrived in East Lansing he was an assistant at Washington State and head coach at Montana. Neither school was considered to be a major court power. Since a great deal of college recruiting depends on the reputation of the school and the personality of the coach, most people figured Magic would choose Michigan.

Still, he wasn't saying anything and that summer after graduating high school, he became a member of a United States team that would play in the Albert Schwitzer Games in Europe. When he returned, he said, he'd announce his decision about a college.

There was great interest in Magic's decision throughout the entire state and when he got off the plane that brought him back from Germany, there was a large crowd waiting for him at the airport. Half of them carried Michigan banners, and the other half were pushing Michigan State. They wouldn't let him forget his hometown for a minute, and indeed he hadn't. Shortly after his return he announced that he would attend Michigan State University. The suspense was over.

"Michigan thought it had a lot more to offer than Michigan State," said Magic, "and in some ways it did. After all, they are on national television and have more basketball prestige, especially in recent years. But I decided to pick the underdog school, since I've always enjoyed being the underdog. Every team I have played on wasn't supposed to win, but we did. Even when I go to the playground I never pick the best players. I'd rather pick guys with less talent, but who are willing to work hard."

The news was greeted with wild enthusiasm at Michigan State and in the Lansing area. The next day when the Michigan State box office opened, one hundred season tickets were sold within the first two hours and before the first game was even played, the arena was sold out, the first time that had ever happened. The Spartans played their home games at Jenison Field House and Magic was no stranger there, having had some of his greatest high school triumphs on that very court.

Magic, of course, wasn't the only good thing that had happened to the Spartan program. Jay Vincent was also going there, plus there was already one outstanding player in the fold. He was junior Greg Kelser, a 6 ft. 7 in. forward who was extremely quick and could seemingly jump to the sky. So it looked as if Coach Heathcote would have a very solid nucleus around which to build a winning team.

It didn't take long for Magic and the Spartans to show they were for real, a force to be reckoned with. In an early season game with Wichita State, Magic was incredible. He had 19 points, 20 rebounds, and nine assists. His size, along with his other attributes, allowed him to do so many things on the court.

He was the team's quarterback, doing the bulk of the ballhandling, even though Heathcote often had two smaller guards in the game at the same time. But the offense always initiated with Magic.

Yet the presence of the other guards allowed him to shift to forward defensively, where he was in a better position to rebound and start the fastbreak. He did this by either firing a quick outlet pass, or by bringing the ball the length of the floor by himself and feeding off to a teammate at the last instant.

Some of his passes were already lifting the lid off the Jenison Field House. He could deliver the ball with zip and accuracy from a variety of positions, often while moving quickly and in midair. He worked especially well with Kelser, who also had tremendous speed, and the two were already perfecting their version of the alley-oop pass, where Kelser would leap high in the air toward the basket and Magic would lob a high pass from wherever he was at the time. Kelser would then catch the ball in the air and in one motion slam-dunk it home. It was an electrifying and effective play, one which could take the heart out of the opposition.

After their early successes in non-conference games, the Spartans prepared to open the Big Ten season against Minnesota. Big Ten play is rough and very competitive, and it's often difficult for one team to really dominate. So the Spartans looked to the game against the Gophers as a barometer for their Big Ten season.

As expected, the game was a tough one. Though Minnesota wasn't expected to be a conference power, they hung tough, with the lead changing hands several times. When it ended, the Spartans had an 87–83 victory and Magic Johnson was once again the best player on the floor. He had scored 31 points, pulled down eight rebounds, and handed off for four assists. He was also tough in the clutch, making 13 of 15 chances from the free throw line. Afterward, he was really excited about the whole team effort.

"I really didn't expect us to be doing this well so soon," he said. "When I came here I figured we'd be the underdog and really have to rise to the occasion. But after this win tonight, I think we can do it, win the Big Ten title."

The team quickly showed they weren't about to rest on their laurels. Two nights later they whipped Wisconsin as Magic had eighteen points, seven rebounds and six assists. He was the season's first Big Ten Player of the Week, and before long began getting the national publicity that would continue right up to the present day. When word began getting out that Michigan State had a 6 ft. 8 in. freshman who played guard, more and more people wanted to see him in action.

In the Spartans first conference road game, Magic put on a real show for the Illinois fans. He had 17 points, 10 assists, eight rebounds, and four steals. By the time the club had played 13 games, they stood at 12-1 and were atop the Big Ten, still unbeaten in conference play.

There were a large number of fine freshman players in 1977-78. Besides Magic and teammate Vincent, there was Gene Banks of Duke, Albert King of Maryland, Cliff Robinson of USC, Herb Williams of Ohio State, and Jeff Ruland of Iona. But as one national magazine put it, Magic was "the brightest member of the Class of '81."

He was also being very successful in the classroom, carrying a 3.4 grade average his first semester at Michigan State. So Magic was more than just a jock who cared about his sport and nothing else. He faced up to his college responsibilities on all levels. Of course, rival coaches weren't talking about his performance in the classroom. In fact, most of them wished he stuck to the classroom, because on the basketball court he was giving them gray hairs.

"Magic is just great," said Illinois Coach Lou Henson. "I've never seen a 6'-8" freshman who can do all the things he can do."

Detroit head man Dave Gaines looked at it in a slightly different light. "Magic had only eleven points against us, but he killed us with something like thirteen assists. Everyone seems to like him and he's just the player Michigan State needed to get its program started again."

There was a definite ring of truth to that. In something like half a season, Magic had become the biggest drawing card in the conference. Besides his skills, he continued to exhibit a joy and enthusiasm for the game that was catching, transmitted to teammates and fans alike. Kevin Smith, a high school rival of Magic's, and a freshman player at the University of Detroit in 1977–78, said this:

"I'm not surprised at anything he does because, like his nickname says, he's magic. Besides his abilities, he's a very special person and he draws people to him like a magnet."

So the Spartans and Magic continued to have an outstanding year, breaking into the top ten and surprising everyone by winning the Big Ten title for the first time since 1959. Hopes were high as they entered the NCAA championship tournament, and they did well in the early rounds. Then in the Midwest Regional final, the team lost to eventual national champ Kentucky, 52–49. But they had nothing to be ashamed of, coming from a losing season to finish 1977-78 with a 25-5 record.

As for the Magic man, he was everything everyone expected, and more. Playing in all 30 Spartan games, he scored 511 points for a 17.0 average, grabbed 237 rebounds, a 7.9 per game clip, and handed off for 222 assists, nearly 7.6 a contest. He was the Spartans' Most Valuable Player, a unanimous all-Big Ten choice, and the only freshman in the country named to a major all-American team.

If there were any criticisms at all, it might have been his 45.8 percent shooting from the floor, giving the impression that Magic didn't shoot that well from the outside, which he didn't at the time. He also had some defensive deficiencies, but often compensated with his size and speed.

"You don't talk about the points Earvin scores, but the points he produces," said Jud Heathcote. "It's not just the baskets and assists, but the first pass that makes the second pass possible. Earvin is aware of scoring, but it's not an obsession with him like it is with so many other players. He just doesn't worry about getting his average every game. He has the ability to control the play without dominating it, and that makes him even more effective."

Magic himself agreed there was much more to his game than just scoring.

"My whole game is court sense," he said. "That means being smart, taking charge, setting up a play, or, if I have to, scoring. The players I've tried to pattern myself after are George Gervin and Doctor J. I can't shoot the way they do, but they're both big, can handle the ball, and they're smooth.

That's what I really like, how smooth they are."

The Spartans had real high hopes in 1978-79. Senior Greg Kesler was a co-captain and the other was Magic, a high honor for a sophomore, but apparently Coach Heathcote still couldn't forget about the pros, for when he announced that Magic would be his co-captain, he added. "This could be his last season here."

Michigan State wasn't a real deep club, but the starting five were solid and there were a couple of subs who wouldn't hurt the club when called upon. Magic and Kelser were the stars, of course, both all-American candidates. Vincent was improving at Center and a solid player. Guard Terry Donnelly was a scrapper and fine defensive player, while forward Mike Brkovich was an excellent shooter. Slender Ron Charles could fill in at both forward and center.

It didn't take the club long to show its striking power. They opened with a game against the touring Russian National team and won it, 76-60. Then they whipped Central Michigan, 71-54, Cal State-Fullerton, 92-89, and Western Michigan, 109-69. With another year's experience, Magic was playing brilliantly, as was Greg Kelser, and the two were a devastating combination.

Then came the team's first real tough game, with perennial top 10 team, North Carolina. It went down to the wire, but the Tar Heels pulled it out, 70-69. After that the club whipped Cincinnati, then played in the Far West Classic, winning the title by whipping Indiana in the finals, 74-57. Wins over Wisconsin and Minnesota followed, giving the club six straight, and they seemed headed for a super season once more.

But suddenly, things began going sour. Two straight Big Ten losses, to Illinois and Purdue, both two-point games, derailed the Spartan express. They rallied to beat Indiana and Iowa, then were whipped by Michigan and Northwestern, losing to the Wolverines by a single point, 49-48, then getting buried by the Wildcats, 83-65. The club had dropped four of six games and seemed in danger of watching its whole season go down the drain.

Magic wasn't faultless in the team's slump. He had been showing some inconsistencies in his own game, not shooting especially well and turning the ball over a few times too many. With three of the four losses coming by a total of five points, there was even some question about Magic's ability to perform in clutch situations. One Detroit sportswriter put it this way:

"Johnson is far from a polished player along the lines of an Oscar Robertson or Jerry West. But he has more raw ability than most of the pro guard prospects now in college. And there are only a handful of NBA guards who can match his potential."

Yet the losses notwithstanding, the pros were still drooling over the Magic man. Witness the remarks of pro scout Al Menendez of the Detroit Pistons, made at the same time the Spartans were losing.

"The things that really make Magic a great player are his unselfishness and his enthusiasm," said Menendez. "You just don't see many young kids with his ability who look to pass the ball first. And his enthusiasm is contagious. He can ignite a team with his attitude."

Spartan guard Terry Donnelly agreed with that

evaluation. "Magic gets the team going," said Donnelly. "He's got a personality like Muhammad Ali. It's classy, not conceited or anything like that. Sometimes he tells jokes while he's running down the floor and he's always smiling and laughing, never a frown on his face. To be like that and to still produce, well, there's no way you could replace that."

Of course, the immediate problem was to get the team out of its slump before they blew the Big Ten title and a possible berth in the NCAA tourney. That's what a coach is for and Heathcote realized he had to make some moves. In recent games, he had been starting Ron Charles at forward with Mike Brkovich coming off the bench. He decided it would be better the other way around, especially because of another change he was about to make.

The coach decided to move Magic up to forward and put Brkovich into the backcourt, a position Charles couldn't play.

"I analyzed our club incorrectly at the start of the season," the coach said. "I thought Earvin could destroy people at guard, but I learned he needs the freedom of being able to set up both inside and outside."

There was still ample opportunity for Magic to handle the ball and to fastbreak, but being up front more gave him added opportunities to score and rebound. The formula seemed to work as the club whipped Ohio State, 84–79, then went about the business of avenging its losses. They began beating everyone in sight, along the way taking Northwestern, Michigan, Purdue, and Illinois, the four Big Ten clubs that had beaten them.

In all, they won ten straight, losing the final regular season game to Wisconsin, 83–81, but by then they had wrapped up their second consecutive conference crown. They ended the regular season with a 21–6 mark and 13–5 Big Ten slate, and were once again ranked among the ten best in the country and given a good chance to make a run at the national championship.

The first game in the tourney was easy. The Spartans whipped Lamar, 95–64, in a cakewalk. The next one, the Mideast Regional semifinals, wouldn't be as easy, as the Spartans had to go against a good Louisiana State ballclub. Tiger coach Dale Brown knew his team couldn't run with the Spartans, so he was hoping they could get an early lead, then slow the pace, maybe even freeze the ball.

For a minute or two it seemed they might have a shot at slowing things up. Playing deliberately, the Tigers took a 5–3 lead and had the ball again. But Kelser intercepted a pass and raced downcourt for a slam-dunk. Seconds later, he did it again, giving the Spartans a 7–5 advantage and igniting the team's running game. From there, Magic took charge, and along with Kelser they buried the Tigers, 87–71, with Magic getting 24 points and 12 assists.

In the Mideast final, the Spartans would have to meet Notre Dame, a very deep club that was ranked number one in the country at times during the season. Coach Digger Phelps was known for juggling a large number of players in and out of the lineup, and when Jud Heathcote looked at the Irish roster, he summed the game up in a single, short sentence.

"Notre Dame goes at you with nine players, and

we come back at you with two."

Even Coach Heathcote was admitting that his one-two punch of Johnson and Kelser held the key to the club's success. Other than that, the Spartans were just an average team at best. And in an attempt to negate the dynamic duo, Coach Phelps planned to put his best defensive player, 6 ft.-7 in. Bill Hanzlik, on Magic.

"If I were Hanzlik, I'd say something about Magic's mother and then hope he'd hit me and get ejected," quipped Kelser.

As for Magic, he sounded a much more somber note. "This is our chance right here. I don't think the club will go this far next year. Kelser is a senior, and as for me, I don't know what I'm going to do about the pros. So this is it."

The opening tip set the tempo of the entire game. Kelser leaped high and got the ball to Magic, who, without looking, flipped it over his head and right on the mark to Brkovich, who raced in for a dunk. The Irish tried to settle down and for a time made a game of it, keeping the score very close.

Then about midway through the first half, Kelser suddenly exploded, scoring seven straight baskets, four of them on passes from Magic. His spurt extended a three-point lead to nine, and after that Notre Dame had to play catch up. The Irish never got closer than seven points, and the Spartans kept running right until the final buzzer, winning it, 80–68, to advance to the Final Four.

Kelser was absolutely brilliant against the Irish, scoring 34 points, while Magic fed off for thirteen assists. Three times the two connected on their patented lob-dunks, as Kelser had six slams in all. After the game he talked about it.

"Magic and I work together extremely well on that play," he said. "A little eye contact is all we need. I know what he's looking for and he knows what I'm looking for. I've been dunking since I was 5'-10" when I was 14. My first was in gym class while we were supposed to be shooting lay-ups. The coach got real mad and made me do ten pushups. But I was so excited I couldn't wait to dunk again. I've loved it ever since and Magic is the perfect guy to team up with."

That was for sure. As Terry Donnelly said, "That's our offense. One passes and the other dunks."

So it was on to the Final Four, which would be played at Salt Lake City, Utah. The other three teams coming in for the showdown were top ranked and unbeaten Indiana State, a surprise club all year long, which featured a one-man wrecking crew, 6 ft. 9 in. forward Larry Bird, who was College Player of the Year; highly ranked DePaul, trying to win it for their 65-year-old coach, Ray Meyer; and a real sleeper team, the University of Pennsylvania, the Ivy League champ which had won the Eastern Regional.

The Spartans would meet Penn in one semifinal, and while highly favored, said they were not going in overconfident or complacent. Meanwhile, Penn's best player, Tony Price, was making noises of his own, saying, "I have no fear of Michigan State. They're just a bunch of dudes who play ball."

Play they did. The Spartans were simply devastating from the opening tap, as Johnson and Kelser simply ran through, around, and over the outgunned Quakers. They broke, and broke, and broke, seemingly scoring every time downcourt. At one point in the first half the score was an embarassing 38-8. It was 50-17 at the half, and from there the Spartans coasted to a 101-67 victory.

Once again the big two were remarkable. Magic had 29 points, ten rebounds, and ten assists, while Kelser finished with 28 points and nine rebounds. The two were looking almost unstoppable.

In the other semifinal, Indiana State just got past DePaul, 76-74, as Bird scored 35 points and grabbed sixteen rebounds. But he was playing with a fractured thumb on his left hand, which caused him to commit eleven turnovers. Michigan State also wasn't 100 percent. Center Vincent had a bad foot and wasn't ready for full-time duty. Still, the excitement was electrifying, and Magic was really caught up in it.

"I'm loving every minute of it," he said. "It's exciting and I'm having a good time, like a kid going to a birthday party. Just being in the Final Four and getting all the attention with your name in all the newspapers all over the country, it's great!"

As usual, Magic was having fun while doing the job. But the Sycamores had won 33 straight, so there was one more big job to be done. The Spartans had won fifteen of their last sixteen games, but they still needed one more.

"We've been a very, very good team the last month," said Kelser. "I feel if we win this one we can say we're a great team."

Terry Donnelly looked at it from the viewpoint of many thousands, the meeting of Magic and Bird, considered the two best players in college ball.

"I almost wish I could sit back and watch it myself," he said. "You can't help but get caught up in a confrontation like this. From what I've seen of Bird, he's not just one bird, he's a whole flock."

Happily, for the Spartans, the game wasn't nearly as close as it was expected to be. Heathcote had designed a variation of the Spartan zone defense which, in effect, put "a man and a half" on Bird, and the Sycamore star was frustrated for most of the game. His bad thumb also seemed to be more of a factor than it had been before.

At the same time, Magic and Kelser began doing their thing, breaking, scoring, and dunking, and they received help from an unexpected source. Terry Donnelly, the guard who wanted to sit back and watch, suddenly got hot. He scored his first basket less than five minutes into the game, a hoop that gave the Spartans a lead they never relinquished. Early in the second half, Donnelly scored his final four points that built the lead up to 16 points.

From there Johnson and Kelser did the rest, as the Spartans won the national championship with a 75–64 victory. They had finally shown they were the best in the land. Magic had led the way with 24 points, while Kelser had 19. And Donnelly, who averaged just 6.6 over the season, had 15 to lend a big hand. Larry Bird had 19, but on seven for 21 shooting, was never a factor.

What a year it had been. Magic was named the tourney's Most Valuable Player and, of course, was a consensus first team all-American. His stats were remarkably consistent with those of his freshman year, a 17.1 point average, 234 rebounds compared with 237 the year before, and 269 assists as opposed to 222 his freshman year. His shooting percentage was 46.8, one point higher than the year before.

Under ordinary circumstances, Magic would still have two more years of college remaining and the only question might be what will he do for an encore? But, of course, with the so-called hardship draft he once again had the option, and as soon as the season ending, the guessing began, as did the forces that were trying to tip his hand in one direction or the other.

For one thing, 1980 was an Olympic year, and no one realized at the time that the United States would end up boycotting the Moscow games for political reasons. So some thought Magic would stay at Michigan State at least one more year in order to play on the Olympic team. Then, perhaps, he would turn pro. Of course, when the talk started, no one knew which NBA team would have the draft right to him.

It was generally assumed that whichever team had the first pick would take him. Larry Bird, of course, was the other big attraction, but he had been picked as a junior eligible by the Boston Celtics the year before, so he was already spoken for.

Magic sat back and listened as the various opinions began rolling in. Teammate Greg Kelser, who himself figured to be a first-round choice, said simply, "If I was in Magic's place, I might leave."

His father, Earvin, Sr., kept a low profile with the press, but indicated in which direction the thinking was headed.

"I always told my son what I thought from the time he was in the sixth grade," said Mr. Johnson.

"But I can't tell him to stay or go. It sure seems as if he can't do any more at Michigan State. They won the Big Ten and they won the NCAA's. What else is left?

"I think if he gets the right offer, he'll go this year, say something like $500,000 for four years. I also think he's as ready as he'll ever be for pro ball."

Magic's high school coach, George Fox, also joined the growing numbers who felt the youngster should go.

"You cannot in good conscience advise Earvin to turn down millions," said Fox. "Anyone who does is selfish and is not looking out for Earvin's best interests."

Charles Tucker, who was again acting as Magic's unofficial advisor, also remained vague, but seemed to indicate that Earvin would turn pro.

"Opportunity comes just once, and if you're not careful you can throw it away quickly. Of course, if Earvin cared only about the money, he'd have been gone last year. Some people still say he won't make it big as a pro. But, heck, he doesn't have to score a point and he can still destroy you."

On the other side of the coin, there were plenty of people who wanted him to stay. Teammate Jay Vincent thought he would, saying, "College basketball is fun and there's nothing better. I don't think Magic should go pro and I don't think he will."

Spartan Athletic Director Joe Kearney was also hoping. "I have a gut feeling that he's going to be here next year, but that's probably based on my stupidity."

Magic's old friends, Jim and Greta Dart, also

wanted him to stay, but they were being realistic.

"It would be nice to have him in Lansing for another two years," Greta Dart said. Then her husband added, "I'm hoping he stays one more year and then lets the Pistons draft him so we can go down and see him play some. But when we saw him walk off the court in Salt Lake City with that net around his neck, we figured we'd probably lose him."

The campaign to get Magic to stay really took some strange dimensions. A big Spartan fan named Pete Secchia took a full page ad in the *Michigan State News* for $1,200 which begged Magic to stay. In part, the ad read: "We've . . . learned in the marketplace of life that a college degree . . . will be with you always."

Through it all, Magic retained an outward calm and a low profile.

"I don't need a lot of opinions," he insisted. "I can listen to myself. When it's time, I'll say."

Earvin's mother seconded that thought. "He's just silent about it," said Christine Johnson. "Then one day, boom, he'll tell us."

Then while all this was going on, Magic found out which team would have first crack at him. It wouldn't be a last place club. (In the NBA, the last place team gets the first draft choice unless it deals away its pick in a trade.) The Los Angeles Lakers had acquired the choice from the lowly New Orleans Jazz, then won a coin toss with the Chicago Bulls for the first pick of the 1979 college crop.

With this knowledge under his belt and after some preliminary contacts with the Lakers, Magic made his decision. He would apply for the NBA hardship draft, thus ending his college career. At age 20, he was ready to become a pro!

Sure enough, when the NBA draft rolled around, the Lakers called the name of Earvin Johnson as the first pick of the league. Now all he'd have to do was reach a contractual agreement with L.A. and he would be starting a whole new life. Magic seemed to be ready to take the plunge with a healthy attitude.

"Heck, I remember when I wouldn't even let myself dream about being all-city," he reminisced. "I made that, but then all-state seemed out of the question because of all those great ballplayers from Detroit. Now I'm going into the NBA with some other great players. I don't think, for instance, that I'm worth as much as Larry Bird. Being honest about it, he's got more experience and honors, and he's also a white superstar. Basketball needs him.

"But when I think of myself in the NBA I know one thing. I'm going to have fun. There's a time for business, a time for school, and a time for fun. Let me put it this way. Things can be happening at a party before I get there, but when I show up they just happen more."

That happened to be an excellent analogy of Magic's court presence. He always made things happen, and usually for the better. But he would be going to a team that was a long-time enigma, a club that played in the country's glamour capital yet seemed to lack that very thing that characterized Los Angeles—glamour and excitement.

The 1978–79 edition of the Lakers was typical of the past few seasons. The team finished with a 47–35 record, but only good for third place in the Pacific Division, behind Seattle and Phoenix. In the playoffs, they barely got past Denver in a best of three mini-series, then put up little more than a brief struggle in losing to Seattle in five games, 4-1, in the Western Conference semi-final. And for awhile, there was no reason to think they would do much better the next year.

Abdul-Jabbar had seemed almost disinterested at times, averaging 23.8 a game, below his usual norm. The next two scorers were Jamaal Wilkes and Adrian Dantley, Wilkes at 18.6 and Dantley at 17.3. The problem was that both were considered small forwards, and when playing together didn't give the big guy much help on the boards. Young Norm Nixon was a speedy point guard and in his second season had averaged 17.1 points a game and was third in the league in assists. But behind him were veterans Lou Hudson, Ron Boone, and Jim Price. All had seen better days. The rest of the team consisted of mediocre veterans and untried youngsters. The mix just wasn't right.

It was obvious that the team needed a real facelift, but doubtful that owner Jack Kent Cooke was willing to do it. He had been having personal problems and was showing little interest in the team. But shortly after the draft, some of Cooke's problems were resolved, and suddenly he stepped in to make a real effort at signing Magic, who was being aided and advised by old friend Dr. Charles Tucker.

Magic, of course, wanted to know a few things about the Lakers, the foremost being whether Kareem Abdul-Jabbar planned to continue playing. When assured that the big guy would be back and undoubtedly finish his career in L.A., the negotiations began in earnest, and they didn't take long. A press conference was soon called and it was announced that Magic had signed a big, five-year pact with the Lakers, a contract that would pay him between $400,000 and $500,000 a year!

Right away there was speculation as to how Magic would do in the pros. The NBA certainly needed him, as well as Larry Bird, who had signed a similar contract with the Celtics. League attendance had been down for a few years, as were the television ratings, and many blamed it on a few main factors. One was the growing moodiness and complacency of the ballplayers. Many of them were getting long-term, no-cut contracts and seemed to put out only when they felt like it. The league was getting a reputation as one in which the players went through the motions until playoff time. Then the intensity re-emerged.

So there was a need for excitement, and Philadelphia 76ers General Manager Pat Williams saw that in Magic, but at the same time sounded a warning.

"I think half of Magic's appeal is his enthusiasm," said Williams, "but you have to remember that happiness and glow and joy often turn to dust in our league."

Magic himself felt he could keep his enthusiasm at a high level for most of the long season. "It's impossible to play hard for 82 games," he said, "but I bet I can do it for at least 70!"

One of the other league problems was the declining franchises in the three most important league cities, New York, Boston, and Los Angeles. That's why NBA officials were so happy with the Lakers getting Magic, the Celtics obtaining Bird, and the New York Knicks drafting a talented, 7 ft. center, Bill Cartwright of San Francisco. So optimism was running high everywhere.

It got even higher in L.A. when, shortly after the signing of Magic, Jack Kent Cooke suddenly sold the team to Dr. Jerry Buss. The new owner was a Ph.D., in chemistry from USC, hence the title Doctor, but he had really made a fortune dealing in Southern California real estate. When he took over the Lakers he decided to do things right.

For starters, he wanted to make his returning players happy. He immediately upgraded the contracts of Wilkes and Nixon, as well as that of Michael Cooper, a second year forward-guard or swing man, who had spent most of his rookie year on the disabled list, but who was expected to contribute heavily in the upcoming season. He also gave Abdul-Jabbar a new contract, calling for about a million dollars a year, plus free use of the L.A. Forum for one night a season for the event of his choosing.

Then Buss went to his general manager, Bill Sharman, and told him to make any player moves he deemed necessary to give the team more balance and depth. Sharman first dealt the talented Dantley, who at 6 ft. 5 in. couldn't play alongside the 6 ft 6 in. Wilkes. He then acquired veteran power forwards Spencer Haywood and Jim Chones, hoping they would fill that most important slot. In addition, the 6 ft 9 in. Haywood and 6 ft 11 in. Chones could both fill in at center if the situation called for it. Sharman also sent some of the other veterans packing and brought in young players who hopefully would develop and contribute.

So when Magic left for his first pro training camp, the Lakers had just four players remaining from the team of a year ago—Abdul-Jabbar, Nixon, Wilkes, and Michael Cooper. All this made the Magic man very happy, but he also knew he'd have to work very hard to fit in with his new teammates.

Everybody had to get acquainted at the Laker camp, since there were so many new faces. Even the coach was new. He was Jack McKinney, who had been an assistant at Milwaukee when Abdul-Jabbar played there and was also an assistant at Portland. It would be his job to put all the pieces together.

In training camp, Magic looked awkward and unsure at first, but then again there were seven new players expected to stick, plus some other rookies and free agents who would eventually be cut. So it was a learning experience for everyone, and Magic explained why his style of play dictated his breaking in slowly and cautiously.

"I felt I had to use the time in training camp to watch my new teammates and try to learn their tendencies," Magic said. "If I'm going to throw a no-look pass, I want to be sure somebody's going to be there to catch it. There were still times when I messed up because I thought somebody would be in a place where they weren't, or because they thought I couldn't see them when they were open. I hit some people in the face at first and I got a lot of turnovers, but I just kept working at it until I got it right."

In the first preseason game of the year, some 15,000 fans showed up to see Magic and the new Lakers as they went up against San Diego. The Clippers controlled the opening tip, but twenty seconds into the game, Magic stole the ball, dribbled downcourt, and scored on a short, eight-foot bank shot. The Magic Johnson era had begun. Minutes later he canned a 22-footer, surprising people who figured he wouldn't shoot much from the outside. There were mistakes, of course, and signs of his inexperience, but Magic looked good.

It was a foregone conclusion that Magic would crack the starting lineup and be playing alongside Nixon, a cat-quick 6 ft. 2 in. playmaker who was a deadly shot from the top of the key and also a fine penetrating guard. In his first two seasons, Nixon was the team's quarterback, doing the brunt of the ballhandling. With Magic on hand, the veteran would often have to defer to the rookie. There was a question whether each man could take his turn working without the ball.

Magic, as usual, quickly won over his new teammates with the magnetism of his personality. He made a special effort to communicate with Nixon, making sure the veteran knew he wanted to work with him and not become a rival or compete for the ball. As a result, the two became fast friends as well as working beautifully together. They didn't have a single problem all year.

"I think I'm getting tight we all the guys," Magic said, as the season drew near. "I'm especially tight with Norm. He looks out for me. I'm also real close with Kareem. I heard all those stories about how difficult he was, how he keeps to himself, how he's this and that. But he's completely different. He'll come in and joke and be real friendly. And, wow, can that man play basketball."

Coach McKinney was also pleased at the way his players were pulling together and also how they'd taken to Magic. He felt it was their talents that were bringing them together.

"Kareem is probably the best offensive weapon

in the game if you get him the ball in close," McKinney said. "So when you put a guy on the court who has a great ability to do that, it's natural that those two are going to become good friends. All the players like Magic. He's a great kid, and they know he's going to deliver."

The Lakers were scheduled to open the 1979–80 season against the San Diego Clippers, with the game set for national television since the Clippers had acquired the services of center Bill Walton. The TV people figured a Walton-Abdul-Jabbar matchup, plus the debut of Magic Johnson would bring high ratings. Unfortunately, Walton was out with a foot injury, but the game turned out to be a great one nevertheless.

In the early going, it was dominated by San Diego guard Lloyd Free, who seemed determined to prove his nickname of "All-World" was justified. Free was hitting long jumpers from all over the court and he propelled the Clippers into a healthy lead.

By the second half the Lakers were playing catch-up, and playing it well. Magic was having a fine game, scoring on a variety of short jumpers and drives, and playing with confidence. He also wasn't afraid to go underneath and mix it up with the big boys.

Then in the final minutes the Lakers got close, tying the game as the clock wound down. With just seconds left, Kareem threw up a sky-hook as the buzzer sounded. It went in! The Lakers had won the game. With the TV cameras honing in, Magic threw his arms around Kareem, a wide smile on his face. It was as if the Lakers had just won the title and as expected, he was providing the kind of excitement and enthusiasm that had been missing from the Lakers for a long time.

Besides that, Magic had scored 26 big points in his first pro game, so his contribution was considerably more than cheerleading. As coach McKinney had said, they all knew he was going to deliver.

"I always get a lot of enjoyment out of life and I want others to get the same thing," Magic said. "When someone pays money for a ticket, I want him to get a show from me. He will, too, because I have to please myself, and if I please myself I'm going to please others."

It was a great start with the promise of more to come. But two games later there was a real scare. The Lakers were playing at Seattle when Magic went up for a rebound and came down to the floor hard. Suddenly, he was writhing in agony, holding his right knee, as a hush came over the crowd. He was helped from the floor and examined by the Seattle team doctor. The diagnosis was devastating.

They said Magic had a tear of the medial collateral ligament in the knee and the preliminary estimate was that he'd be out some six weeks. And with knee injuries, with the specter of possible surgery, one never knows. Careers have ended with ligament tears. Everyone hated to see it happen to Magic.

But then an amazing turnaround occurred. A subsequent closer examination revealed that the ligament wasn't torn. The injury was merely a strain, and everyone breathed a collective sigh of relief. Magic missed just three games, and when he returned he promptly scored 26 points against Kansas City.

"I never thought all this would happen to me," Magic said. "Seems like yesterday when I was shooting for all-city. But the strangest thing is, now that I'm here in the NBA, it feels totally natural, like this is where I always belonged."

The Lakers certainly weren't complaining. They were winning, and doing it with more of a flare than anytime in recent years. Bill Sharman's moves that brought in Haywood and Chones were paying dividends, as the club was being pushed around a lot less underneath, and if it got real rough under there, Magic was quick to jump in and lend a hand.

In a close game against Phoenix early in the year, the score was tied with less than 30 seconds left and the Lakers called a timeout. Coach McKinney began describing a play that would get the ball up front to Wilkes. Rookie or no, Magic spoke up and said why he thought he should get the shot. McKinney agreed, then held his breath as Magic was fouled, and won the game with a pair of free throws.

"The first thing Magic brought us was enthusiasm and excitement and I think that has been infectious," McKinney said. "We knew the kind of passer he was and envisioned him as a leader and ball-handler, with the ability to get the ball into Kareem. We never really thought of him as a scorer, but he played some ball in a summer league here and was getting thirty or forty points a game. That's when we began to realize the full extent of his potential."

After thirteen games, the club had a 9-4 record when a real disaster did happen. Coach McKinney took a fall from a bicycle near his home and suffered a severe head injury. For awhile, doctors feared for his life. He passed the first crisis, but the recovery period would be a long one. Assistant Paul Westhead, in his first year in the NBA, was appointed interim coach. Now the question was would the Laker's balance and harmony be affected by the coaching change?

Fortunately, it wasn't. Westhead quickly showed he was an able tactician, but more importantly, he could communicate with his players and they quickly developed a respect for him. So McKinney's unfortunate accident didn't really disrupt the flow of the team.

By the time Magic had played his first twelve games with the Lakers he was really earning his keep. His scoring average was at 20.3, and surprisingly, he was hitting on 55.5 percent of his shots, tops for any guard in the league. Who said he couldn't shoot? And soon after that he completed a three-game span in which he scored 89 points, took down 35 rebounds, and handed off for 34 assists. They were stats reminiscent of his days at Michigan State and for that effort, he was named NBA Player of the Week.

Of course, every game didn't produce a super effort. There were some off nights when Magic didn't have the touch. He still made some mistakes on defense and tended to turn the ball over too often. But the Lakers learned to compensate. Abdul-Jabbar was acting like a rookie himself and producing his best all-around season in several years, as was Jamaal Wilkes, also playing with renewed intensity. Chones was proving a valuable acquisition, having moved into the starting lineup and giving the club a steadying influence.

And when Magic wasn't doing the job in the backcourt, Nixon was. Magic's presence had elevated his game, if anything. He was scoring as well as he had before Magic's arrival and joining Magic in the top ten in the league's assist column.

By midseason, the Lakers were battling Seattle and Phoenix for the Pacific Division lead. Magic had caught on everywhere. In fact, the league fans voted him a starting berth on the West all-star squad, the first time a rookie had started the All-Star Game since 1969. Some coaches and writers said that Magic didn't really deserve that honor, that he had just won a popularity contest. But Laker assistant Pat Riley didn't agree.

"Everybody thinks Magic is up there riding on the wagon, throwing roses to everyone," Riley said. "But I'll tell you what, he pulls the wagon a lot. When the game is on the line, he's in the action. He's not really a guard or a forward. He's what you would just call a player, a complete player."

Paul Westhead also commented on Magic's versatility, calling him "a point guard who is a slick passer and also a power forward who plays like a thug."

In late February, the Lakers defeated the Denver Nuggets as Magic scored 30, prompting Westhead to again comment on the rookie's many attributes.

"If you look at his nickname you would think that all he does is make fancy passes," the coach said. "But he's as much a bread-and-butter guard as he is a passer. He'll take the ball down the lane in traffic and he'll also rebound. That's why he's so respected by his teammates. He gets down in the trenches, too, but he can still make the Bob Cousy-type pass."

Indeed, Magic was moving up front more as the season progressed. The development of second-year man Michael Cooper, a wiry, 6 ft. 6 in. swing man who was excelling on defense, allowed Westhead the luxury of playing three guards, two of whom could easily go up front. That gave the team added depth and maneuverability.

By March, the Lakers had surged into first place in a continuing dogfight with Seattle. Magic was showing even more consistency. His scoring average was a shade over eighteen points a game, he was getting nearly 7.5 assists, and still shooting 53 percent from the field. His seven rebounds a game made him the best rebounding guard in the league.

"I think Magic has led us," Kareem said. "He has really improved since the beginning of the year. He's playing basically the same game, but he's getting smarter and throwing the ball away less."

Jim Chones echoed those sentiments. "If he playing great?" exclaimed Chones. "The last fifteen games he's been doing everything. He certainly makes it much easier for me and Kareem with his rebounding. I love it. He's really made progress and is now a major threat."

Magic was doing well on a number of fronts by now. With his small coterie of friends and advisors still guiding him, he was beginning to do commercials and pick up endorsements. His business affairs were being managed by a firm in Chicago which made careful, safe investments, and along with his friends from home, made sure he wasn't taking on too much or spending too much time away from the game. That always came first. In fact, he turned down a number of things, including a chance to do some guest shots on television because of the schedule.

He was also careful not to get mixed up with the

wrong people or be taken in by those who like to hang on the coattails of celebrities. Yet he was still able to take in and enjoy his rather glamourous surroundings.

"It's nice and it's different," he said. "I guess it's like you say—Hollywood. It's something you always dream about and now I've had the opportunity to experience it, to get out and really meet the stars. I've already met people like Muhammad Ali, Richard Pryor, Jane Fonda, and Jayne Kennedy. I've been invited to private parties with all the big celebs. When I'm standing there and talking to them, I just can't wait to call home and tell everybody about it.

"I've been down to the set of 'The White Shadow' and had a chance to meet all the people from 'Happy Days.' So I've been able to do things, meet stars, and feel good about it. But the most full will still be going home and telling everyone about everything."

A kid at heart, why not? The only place where he was surely mature beyond his years was on the court. In a late season game against Cleveland he popped in 24 points, had 16 rebounds, and 12 assists. When he produced an all around game like that he was close to incredible. After that one, Paul Westhead came up to him with a stat sheet and deadpanned:

"Sixteen boards, Magic. Hey, you're supposed to be a guard!"

To that, Magic smiled broadly and quipped, "I'll try to do better next game, coach."

So the long season wound down with the Lakers finishing very strong. The team had picked up veteran forward Mark Landsberger for more rebounding insurance and now had eight solid players who were all contributing, and the youngsters who didn't see that much action. The team had overhauled Seattle in the closing weeks and finished atop the Pacific Division.

The Lakers' final mark was 60-22, second best in the entire league. The Celtics had finished at 61-21, with Magic's old rival, Larry Bird, also having a brilliant rookie season and helping turn the Celts around. The Philadelphia 76ers closed at 59-23, and the Seattle Supersonics at 55-26. These four teams were the favorites as the league got ready for the long playoff schedule.

Kareem once again led the Lakers in scoring with a 24.8 mark, sixth best in the league. He had completed a brilliant season, one that would bring him an unprecedented sixth Most Valuable Player Award. Wilkes also had his finest season with a 20.0 point scoring average. Magic came next, netting 1,387 point in 77 games for an 18.0 average, and he was followed closely by Nixon's 17.6. Chones' 10.6 rounded out an explosive and balanced attack.

In addition to his scoring, Magic grabbed 596 rebounds, best of any guard in the league, and handed out 563 assists, a 7.3 average, good for seventh in the league. Nixon, by the way, had 642 assists, a 7.8 average, fourth best in the league. That showed just how well he and Magic worked together in the Laker backcourt. They both handed out the goodies and scored at about the same clip. Of course, all this would be meaningless if the club did its annual swan song in the playoffs. So they began gearing up early.

Many people were looking for a Laker-Celtic

final, for that would be a natural for a Johnson-Bird matchup, and the NBA and TV people could have a publicity bonanza with that one, the two rivals for the NCAA title a year earlier hooking up once again. But both clubs would have to get there first.

Because they won their division, the Lakers had a bye in the first round. But there were problems while waiting for the winner of the Phoenix-Kansas City mini-series. Kareem had come down with severe migraine headaches, something he had experienced before, but these were especially painful and for a time his availability was in doubt.

It turned out that the Phoenix Suns would be the Lakers' opponents, and when the teams took to the court for game one in L.A., the big guy was in there. In fact, he led the way with 30 points as the Lakers made it look easy, 119-110. Nixon had 26, Wilkes 19, and Magic 13 in a balanced attack.

The second game was the toughest of the series. It was a see-saw struggle all the way and tied at 120 at the end of regulation. The Lakers won it when Nixon hit a jumper with 20 seconds left in overtime, then added a free throw in a 131-128 win. Paul Westphal led Phoenix with 37, while the Lakers again showed balance among their big four scorers. Kareem had 32, Wilkes and Nixon 26 each, and Magic 25.

Game three saw the Lakers come from behind in the fourth period to win, 108-105. They just seemed to have too much firepower and were too quick for the Suns. Phoenix did manage to win a fourth game, but then the Lakers closed it out with a 126-101 victory. With a 4-1 series victory, the Lakers now prepared to meet the defending NBA champion Seattle Supersonics in the Western Conference finals.

The Sonics would be tough. They had a great backcourt in Dennis Johnson and Gus Williams, with Downtown Freddie Brown coming off the bench. Jack Sikma was a rugged center, while Lonnie Shelton and John Johnson were a good combo at forward. Plus the team had depth and an outstanding bench coach in Lenny Wilkens. And as defending champions they had the pride that would drive them again.

Game one seemed to bring out that pride. Playing in the L.A. Forum, Seattle kept it close all the way, then came on in the final seconds to win it, 108-107. Freddie Brown had 34 points and Williams, 28, showing just how potent the Sonic backcourt was. Kareem led L.A. as usual with 26, while Magic had 19. The growing pressure of the playoffs was not affecting him at all.

Right away the Lakers were faced with a big game. They couldn't afford to lose two straight on their home court. And they didn't, coming on to win with a big third quarter, 108-99, knotting the series at one-each. After that the Lakers really showed their superiority. They won game three in Seattle, and they broke the Sonics heart in game four.

Seattle seemed to be putting it together at last, and took a huge, 21-point lead halfway into the third period. But suddenly they died, couldn't do a thing right, and the Lakers went to a strategy that was quickly becoming invaluable. Michael Cooper checked in at guard and Magic moved to power forward. Those three, along with Wilkes and Kareem, ran the Sonics into the ground. They ended up winning, 98–93, as Magic tied Kareem for a team high of 13 rebounds.

After that, it was just a matter of time. L.A. won the fifth game to take their second straight series by a 4–1 count. Now they were in the finals, where the team had blown it so many times before. This time, they vowed, it would be different.

There was one slight disappointment. Fans would not be seeing a Johnson-Bird confrontation after all. The Celtics had been eliminated with relative ease by the 76ers. So L.A. would be meeting Philadelphia and their great superstar forward, Julius Erving.

The Sixers were strong in other places, as well. Young Darryl Dawkins could be a ferocious force at center, though he lacked consistency. Seven-footer Caldwell Jones was a marvelous defensive player who could swing from forward to center and effectively guard smaller men. The backcourt of Maurice Cheeks and Lionel Hollins was also very steady, and the bench led by Bobby Jones, Steve Mix, and Henry Bibby could do the job. It would be a very tough series.

Game one was played in Los Angeles before a sellout crowd of 17,505 noisy fans. For the first half the game was close, the score tied at 53–all at the end of two, both teams playing very well. But in the third quarter, Magic and Nixon got the Lakers running, and it threw the Sixers game off. Kareem was again the focal point with his sky hooks and fine defensive work. The Lakers outscored the Sixers by a 31–17 count in the third, then coasted home with a 109–102 victory.

Kareem was awesome with 33 points, 14 rebounds, five assists, and six blocked shots. Nixon and Wilkes were also over 20 points, while Magic had 16 and ten assists. For Philly, the Doctor had just 20 points and young Dawkins fouled out after just eighteen minutes of action. The Lakers certainly looked like the better team in this one.

Game two proved just the opposite. Philly came out firing and wouldn't let the Lakers get untracked. They led, 31–21, at the quarter, 59–41 at the half, and 89–71 at the end of three. It seemed all but wrapped up. But early in the fourth period Magic hit two straight fastbreak baskets and the Lakers suddenly awakened. They went to the three-guard offense with Cooper and were off to the races.

They kept running and Kareem kept hitting his sky hook as the margin narrowed and narrowed. The fans at the Forum went wild as the Lakers miraculously narrowed the lead to one with just seconds left. But Caldwell Jones hit a short jump hook, and Nixon's three-point try missed. Philly had won it, 107–104, to tie the series, but the Lakers had given them a scare and perhaps even took a moral victory of sorts.

Now the scene shifted back to Philly, where more than 18,000 fans jammed into the Spectrum to root the Sixers home. By winning game two, Philly had taken the so-called home court advantage away from the Lakers. If they could take the next two in their building, they would be in a very commanding position. In their favor was the fact that the Lakers hadn't won a single game at the Spectrum since 1975.

The Lakers were aware of all this, so they took it right to the Sixers, going to the boards with a vengeance and completely dominating the Sixers big men. That was the difference in the early going, as the Lakers jumped to a 31-18 first period lead. From there, the outcome was never in doubt. It was a particularly easy, 111-101 victory, as L.A. didn't take long to negate their loss at home.

They had outrebounded the Sixers, 56-37, a huge edge for a title game, or any game. Kareem again led the way with 33 points and 14 rebounds. Nixon had 22, Wilkes 19, Magic 16, and he also had time to go underneath for 11 rebounds.

In game four, the momentum swung back the other way. The Lakers had been so dominant in three, now it seemed the Sixers were taking their turn. Caldwell Jones had a big game defensively on Kareem, and Darryl Dawkins was doing his thing from the key. The Lakers had a 51-49 lead at the half, but Philly took command in the third period and hung on for a 105-102 win, tying the series once more and sending it back to L.A. for game five.

There was one difference emerging, however. When the Lakers were on their game they would win fairly easily. But when the Sixers seemed to have the upper hand, they'd still have to struggle. In the fourth game, the Lakers still won the battle of the boards, 49-34, and Magic had a big game with 28 points, nine rebounds, and nine assists. He was continuing to play outstanding basketball in a pressure-packed situation.

Game five turned out to be one of the great ones in NBA playoff history. It started innocently enough, the Lakers taking a 25-22 lead after one. But it was a pivotal game and both clubs knew it. Soon, the intensity picked up. The Sixers began scoring well inside, with Erving and Dawkins leading the way, and they took the lead in the second period and went in at the half with a 53-50 advantage.

Magic was not playing that well in game five. He seemed to be struggling a bit, committing too many turnovers, and he was having a poor shooting night. But at the beginning of the third period, he and his teammates picked up the pace, and once again the game was very close. With four and a half minutes left in the session, Kareem scored on a finger-roll, giving the Lakers a 69-67 lead. But as he turned to go upcourt, he stumbled after colliding with Lionel Hollins.

Suddenly the big guy was limping, and limping badly. He tried to go on, but thirty seconds later there was a timeout. He had to leave the game. A hush settled over the crowd. What if he didn't return? This was the Sixers' big chance.

Philly reacted to the big guy's absence by putting a big club on the floor and trying to get the boards. The Lakers responded by running . . . and it paid off. With Kareem out, L.A. increased its lead to 81-73 at the end of three. At the buzzer, Kareem reappeared, his ankle heavily taped, and he was still limping, but he was out there for the final session, determined to give it a go.

Though the big guy was in pain, once he was in position he could still shoot. A sky hook brought the lead to 89-77 Lakers, with just 9:01 left. That's when Julius Erving, the Doctor, took over, something he hadn't done too often in the series. He asked for the ball, got it, and preceeded to show he was still the most dynamic forward in the game, making some unbelievable shots that the Lakers just couldn't stop.

Almost singlehandedly, the Doctor brought the Sixers back into the game. It was reminiscent of his days with the New York Nets of the ABA. The Lakers knew he was coming, but they couldn't keep the Doctor from operating. With 43 seconds left, Julius made a pair of free throws that tied the game at 103-103.

Now the Lakers had the ball and a very important possession. It went to Magic. He lobbed it beautifully over the outstretched arms of Dawkins, right to Kareem, who stuffed and was fouled by Erving. It was a big play, the free throw making it 106-103. Philly then missed a desperation three-pointer, and the Lakers got a last-second hoop to win it, 108-103, despite 36 points from Erving, who had scored 15 of his team's final 20.

Kareem had been outstanding, with forty points of his own and fifteen rebounds. Magic had a spotty game, with four of thirteen shooting from the floor and fourteen points. He also committed ten turnovers. But because of his great overall skills, he still contributed, nailing down fifteen big rebounds, and passing for ten assists, including the key lob to Kareem. There were just so many ways he could hurt you.

But the big question now was Kareem's availability for game six. It didn't take long to find out. The ankle had swelled and he wouldn't make the trip back to Philly. The Lakers would have to play the sixth game without him and if they lost, which everyone expected, they could just hope he'd be ready for a seventh and final game.

Almost everyone assumed that Jim Chones would move into the center slot, with perhaps Magic moving to forward and Cooper starting at guard, or even Mark Landsberger moving into a starting role up front. But before the game Coach Westhead announced that his starting center would be . . . Magic Johnson!

It was a bold move, playing Magic at center on offense, then having him switch to forward on defense and play seven-foot Caldwell Jones.

"I played center in high school," Magic quipped, "and I've even taken a few hook shots in my time." When someone asked if they were sky hooks, referring to Kareem's pet shot, Magic replied, "No, of course not. They're magic hooks."

He also returned to a theme he had used when talking to the press years ago.

"I like being the underdog," he said. "There's nothing we can do about the situation; we can't turn around and go home. Anyway, I kind of like the idea of everyone thinking that we're not going to be able to win."

Coach Westhead also figured his team had a shot. He talked about his rookie's cool when told about the switch of positions.

"When I told him he was the center, he just said, 'Oh, that's nice.' Then when we boarded the flight to Philly, he sits down in Kareem's seat, which is always the first seat on the plane. Then he turns around in my direction and gives me a big wink, as if to say, 'Hey, coach, if I'm gonna play The Man's position, then I'm gonna sit in his seat, too.' He was cool, all right."

It was obvious at the outset that the Lakers were sky high, determined to compensate for Kareem's absence. They jumped off to a 7-0 lead and were dominating play. Suddenly, Magic began performing miracles at center. He scored thirteen first quarter points, including one on a hook shot, and another on a brilliant layup, which he delayed until big Dawkins had committed himself and was coming down again. He made five of his six shots from the floor as the Lakers had a 32-29 lead after one.

In the second period the Sixers rallied, but the Lakers wouldn't let them get away. Magic continued to play brilliantly in the middle and underneath. A rookie? Hard to believe. By halftime it was a 60-60 tie, as Magic had already scored 22 points, and he later remarked:

"We went into the locker room saying, 'We're right where we want to be. Let's go out and do it.' "

That they did. The Lakers returned to the floor and promptly ran off fourteen straight points, to go up, 74-60. Philly tried to rally, but at the end of three could only close to 93-83. Jamaal Wilkes had the hot hand, scoring sixteen points in period three.

Philly did make a run in the final session, closing to 103-101, with 5:11 left. But then Magic scored on an offensive rebound. Minutes later both he and Wilkes hit and were fouled, completing three-point plays. Then Magic scored again and it was 113-103. From there, it was a matter of playing out the clock. The Lakers did it in fine style, winning it, 123-107, without Kareem. They were champions of the world!

Wilkes had one of his greatest games, with 37 points, but it was the Magic man who really lit up the skies. Responding to all the pressure, the wondrous rookie had a career high 42 points, on 14 of 23 from the field and 14 of 14 from the foul line. He had seven assists and pulled down a game high fifteen rebounds. During the Lakers' run of fourteen points at the beginning of the third period, Magic had four points, three rebounds, three assists, and two steals during a three and one-half minute span. He was nearly a one-man wrecking crew.

When it ended, it was announced that Magic had been named the MVP of the series.

"Beautiful, this is just beautiful," was all he could say. "We did it for the big guy. We did it for Kareem."

It was beautiful, all right, a storybook end to a year long odyssey that saw Magic go from the NCAA title to the NBA title in one big magic swoop. And while the Magic man was basking in the glory, others couldn't say enough about his play.

"It's hard to put a label on what he does because he does everything so well," said Julius Erving, who should know. "It's also hard to envision what he'll turn into after a few years under his belt, when he knows what he's doing." The Doctor laughed at that last remark.

Sixers coach Billy Cunningham was also a believer. "There's never been a guard who can rebound like Magic," Cunningham said. "He's 20 years old and he's going to be another Oscar Robertson-Jerry West type player. Only better, because of the way he rebounds."

Magic's accomplishments in so short a time have been truly amazing. There's little doubt that he's the guy who lit a fire under the Lakers. The talent was there, but he brought it to life with his enthusiasm for the game and willingness to play hard, night after night, giving it his all and not being merely satisfied to go through the motions and pick up his paycheck.

He showed just what a 20-year-old kid could do, given the talent and the attitude to make it work. Playing under all kinds of pressure he responded, rising to new heights when he had to, like Kareem, and Erving, and those other very special few. But perhaps there is one difference between Magic and the rest, a quality that he hopefully will never lose.

Magic Johnson has fun. Even in the most critical of situations he's enjoying himself, secure in the knowledge that he's competing in a sport he loves and can play. And, that, Magic Johnson fully appreciates.

STATISTICS

Julius Erving

YEAR	TEAM	G	—2-Point— FGM-FGA	PCT.	—3-Point— FGM-FGA	PCT.	FTM-FTA	PCT.	REB.	PTS.	AVE.
1969–70	UMass	25	238–468	.509	———	——	167–230	.726	522	643	25.7
1970–71	UMass	27	286–609	.470	———	——	155–206	.752	527	727	26.9
College Totals		52	524–1077	.486	———	——	322–436	.739	1049	1370	26.3
1971–72	Virginia	84	907–1810	.501	3–16	.188	467–627	.745	1319	2290	27.3
1972–73	Virginia	71	889–1780	.499	5–24	.208	475–612	.776	867	2268	31.9
1973–74	New York	84	897–1742	.515	17–43	.395	454–593	.766	899	2299	27.4
1974–75	New York	84	885–1719	.515	29–87	.333	486–608	.799	914	2343	27.9
1975–76	New York	84	915–1770	.517	34–103	.330	530–662	.801	925	2462	29.3
ABA Totals		407	4493–8821	.509	88–273	.322	2412–3102	.778	4924	11662	28.7
1976–77	Phila	82	685–1373	.499	———	——	400–515	.777	695	1770	21.6
1977–78	Phila	74	611–1217	.502	———	——	306–362	.845	481	1528	20.6
1978–79	Phila	78	715–1455	.491	———	——	373–501	.745	564	1803	23.1
1979–80	Phila	78	838–1614	.519	4–20	.200	420–534	.787	576	2100	26.9
NBA Totals		312	2849–5659	.503	4–20	.200	1499–1912	.784	2316	7201	23.1

Larry Bird

YEAR	TEAM	G	—2-Point— FGM-FGA	PCT.	—3-Point— FGM-FGA	PCT.	FTM-FTA	PCT.	REB.	PTS.	AVE.
1976–77	ISU	28	375–689	.544	————		168–200	.840	373	918	32.8
1977–78	ISU	32	403–769	.524	————		153–193	.793	369	959	30.0
1978–79	ISU	34	376–707	.532	————		221–266	.831	505	973	28.6
College Totals		94	1154–2165	.533	————		542–659	.822	1247	2850	30.3
1979–80	Boston	82	693–1463	.474	58–143	.406	301–360	.836	852	1745	21.3
NBA Totals		82	693–1463	.474	58–143	.406	301–360	.836	852	1745	21.3

Moses Malone

YEAR	TEAM	G	—2-Point— FGM-FGA	PCT.	—3-Point— FGM-FGA	PCT.	FTM-FTA	PCT.	REB.	PTS.	AVE.
1974–75	Utah	83	591–1034	.572	0–1	.000	375–591	.635	1209	1557	18.8
1975–76	St. Louis	43	251–488	.514	0–2	.000	112–183	.612	413	614	14.3
ABA Totals		126	842–1522	.553	0–3	.000	487–774	.629	1622	2171	17.2
1976–77	Bf-Hous.	82	389–810	.480	———	———	305–440	.693	1072	1083	13.2
1977–78	Houston	59	413–828	.499	———	———	318–443	.718	886	1144	19.4
1978–79	Houston	82	716–1325	.540	———	———	599–811	.739	1444	2031	24.8
1979–80	Houston	82	778–1549	.502	0–0	.000	563–783	.719	1190	2119	25.8
NBA Totals		305	2296–4512	.509	0–0	.000	1785–2477	.721	4592	6377	20.9

Magic Johnson

YEAR	TEAM	G	—2-Point— FGM-FGA	PCT.	—3-Point— FGM-FGA	PCT.	FTM-FTA	PCT.	REB.	PTS.	AVE.
1977–78	Mich State	30	175–382	.458	———		161–205	.785	237	511	17.0
1978–79	Mich State	32	173–370	.468	———		202–240	.842	234	548	17.1
College Totals		62	348–752	.463			363–445	.816	471	1059	17.1
1979–80	L.A.	77	503–949	.530	7–31	.226	374–462	.810	596	1383	18.0
NBA Totals		77	503–949	.530	7–31	.226	374–462	.810	596	1383	18.0